Just One Thing On Top Of Another

A Comedy in Two Acts

By

MARTHA ROBINSON

NEW PLAYWRIGHTS' NETWORK
35, SANDRINGHAM ROAD,
MACCLESFIELD,
CHESHIRE SK10 1QB

First Published January 1973

Made and printed in Great Britain by
Tills, Macclesfield, Cheshire.

CAST

WILLIAM TENNANT	Bill to his wife. A Charge Hand Toolmaker in his mid forties. What little belief he had in himself has disappeared through the humiliation of being out of work.
JOAN TENNANT	his charming wife, about forty. She is an efficient housewife and mother, so used to ordering her husband's life that she believes he cannot do without her.
VICTORIA TENNANT	'Viki' to the family. She is 17 and just like her mother.
SAMANTHA TENNANT	age 15, known as Sammy. She has an unusually good brain. Is going through the cynical stage.
MRS PASMORE	Joan's mother. A bossy widow in her sixties.
DELIA JONES	in her late thirties, an attractive woman, recently widowed. She can turn most situations to her own use.
CHRIS MAITLAND	Viki's boy friend and slave, age 18.
MISS HATTON	in her mid thirties, a schoolteacher at the local Comprehensive.
MR. WEEKS	estate agent in his sixties. A very large, jovial man.

The entire action takes place in the open-plan living room cum kitchen of the Tennant's house somewhere in the Midlands

Time: The Present

ACT 1.   Scene 1. Breakfast time one March morning
            Scene 2. The same afternoon
            Scene 3. A week later about 5 p.m.

ACT 11.   Scene 1. About fifteen minutes later
            Scene 2. A week later, afternoon.
            Scene 3. Two days later, morning.

PRODUCTION NOTES

There are a number of domestic objects to be handled: it would be advisable to use plastic if possible. At the end of Scene I. Act I have a plastic basin in the sink so that all the washing up can be lifted and carried out without noise.

In Act II, Scene I. fade the daylight gradually during the love scene so that it ends in semi-darkness. CUE for table light to be switched on: DELIA: I heard the door. CUE for overhead light to be switched on: MRS PASMORE: You again. . . . .

The stairs must be strong enough for heavy footsteps to be clearly heard and practical for running up and down.

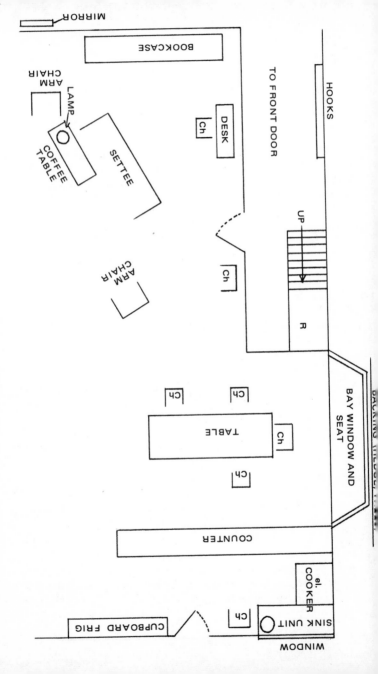

JUST ONE THING ON TOP OF ANOTHER

ACT ONE

SCENE 1

*The open-plan living-room and kitchen of the Tennants'
modern house somewhere in the Midlands.*

Time: The present.

*The kitchen area is L. separated from the living-room by a counter.
Door to side exit extreme L. Door to front hall up R. When this
door is open stairs can be glimpsed back L. The front door is
somewhere back R. A row of coat hooks are on back wall. The
living-room has a bow window up L. Dining area up C. by counter.*

*The living-room contains a modern suite of settee and two arm
chairs, a coffee table, desk and chair, dining-table and five
matching chairs, and a bookcase. The dividing counter has small
drawers over cupboards one drawer containing cutlery etc. one
cupboard a bottle of sherry and glasses.*

*The kitchen has a sink unit with window over it, el. cooker and
kettle. There is a kitchen chair by side door and a wall cupboard
with built-in frig. down L.*

The family, consisting of mother JOAN, father BILL and two daughters VIKI (Victoria, 17) and SAMANTHA (15) are seated, finishing breakfast. BILL is reading a letter. His wife watches him while pretending to be drinking her tea. He drops the letter, picks up another and starts to open it.

JOAN. Nothing, dear?

BILL. No. The usual brush off — sorry the vacancy has been filled.

SAMANTHA. Bad luck, Dad.

BILL. *(examining second letter)* This seems to be from your school.

SAMANTHA. Is it?

VIKI. What about?
    (VIKI gets up and comes round to peer over her father's shoulder)

BILL. They want our permission for the girls to attend a sex education film.

JOAN. Of course. We're not fuddy-duddies.

BILL. *(reading)* Well, listen to this — there's a showing for parents the evening before. What do you make of that?

SAMANTHA. Quite right too. Most parents know nothing.
    (BILL and JOAN laugh)

BILL. How right you are, Sammy. But I'm darned if I want to go.

VIKI. Why not?

BILL. I might be shocked.

SAMANTHA. You would, darling Daddy.

JOAN. What evening is that then?

BILL. Next Thursday.

JOAN. It's my pottery evening. *(struck by a thought)* It isn't that ghastly film the papers have been going on about?

VIKI. Yes, it is. But you know what the papers are.

SAMANTHA. Anything for a headline.

JOAN. All the same — perhaps I ought to give up the class and go. . . . .
    (SAMANTHA and VIKI exchange glances)

SAMANTHA. I shouldn't bother, Mum. Celia Green says it's

all right.

BILL. And which of your many knowledgeable friends is Celia Green?

SAMANTHA. Her father is the barber at the Men's Parlour.

JOAN. And how would he know?

SAMANTHA. Alderman Hodgkins told him he'd seen it and it's O.K.

BILL. Oh. Who are we to disagree with Alderman Hodgkins?

JOAN. Well. . . . so long as you both remember *we* do not belong to the permissive society.

VIKI. As if we could forget. . . . .

(VIKI aims a kiss at her father's cheek and misses. She blows her mother a kiss and moves to the hall door.)

JOAN. Is Chris calling for you, Viki?

VIKI. I expect so.

JOAN. It's marvellous of him to call for you now that he's no longer at school.

SAMANTHA. What's marvellous about it? He passes our door on the way to his job.

JOAN. Does he carry your books?

VIKI. Why ever should he? He never did before.

JOAN. *(sighs)* Things have changed. When I was at school, one's boy friend always carried one's books.

VIKI. See you. *(She exits)*

SAMANTHA. But *one* doesn't expect such discriminatory gestures now, Mum. One is equal with *one's* friends, male or female.

BILL. And that puts *us* in our place!

JOAN. *(bristling)* Not at all. Courtesy to anyone weaker is not discrimination. Women are not as strong as men.

SAMANTHA. *(getting up)* I am. I floored Harry the other day.

JOAN. Harry — the school bully? Samantha, you didn't.

SAMANTHA. I did. Winded him.

BILL. Good for you, Sammy.

JOAN. Please, Bill — that's not the way a girl of fifteen should behave.

(SAMANTHA crosses to hall door)

SAMANTHA. If a boy of fifteen can behave like that, why not a girl? *(She exits)*

JOAN. Oh. . . bye-bye dear. *(sighs)* Will she never stop being a tomboy?

BILL. *(fondly)* Sammy's all right. She's got brains too.

JOAN. I only wish she hadn't got Women's Lib. so badly.

(JOAN rises and starts to collect the dishes and put them on the counter. BILL scrutinises his paper closely, takes a biro and marks something.)

JOAN. What are you doing today, Bill?

BILL. The usual — nothing.

JOAN. The garden needs attention — and there's the guttering —

BILL. Yes. I know.

(There is a pause. JOAN continues to clear the table)

JOAN. Any possible jobs in the paper today?

BILL. Well. . . . . there's one in Birmingham looks promising —

JOAN. Birmingham! That's too far.

BILL. And an even better one at Dagenham.

JOAN. That's out of the question. No sense in applying for either of those.

(The front door is heard to open and a boy's voice calls out)

CHRIS. *(off)* Viki?

VIKI. *(off)* Yes. Coming.

(The front door bangs SAMANTHA comes in, school blazer and beret on, case of books in hand.)

SAMANTHA. *(crossing to her father)* 'Bye Dad. *(She kisses him and waves to her mother)* 'Bye, Mum.

JOAN. Have a good day, dear.

BILL. 'Bye, Sammy.

(SAMANTHA exits. Front door opens and shuts)

JOAN. I wish you wouldn't call her Sammy.

BILL. She likes it.

JOAN. It encourages her to think of herself as a boy.

BILL. She ought to have been.

JOAN. Nonsense. She'll grow into a woman, just as Viki did.

BILL. Well, it hardly matters what they grow into these days.
They all look the same.

JOAN. We *are* funny this morning!
*(JOAN walks round into the kitchen area and starts packing
washing into the kitchen sink.)*

JOAN. You're not thinking of applying for one of those jobs you
mentioned, are you?

BILL. They're not as good as the one in Southampton. I thought
that was a fair offer.

JOAN. Fair offer, indeed! It was almost half your old salary and
not using your special skill.

BILL. *(quietly)* I was made redundant nearly a year ago, Joan.

JOAN. Things are looking up.

BILL. The only thing that's up is unemployment.

JOAN. The tide will turn.

BILL. *(low)* So will the worm.

JOAN. *(sharply)* What did you say?

BILL. I said 'how about Birmingham?'

JOAN. Bill, you know how I feel.
(JOAN comes round the counter and sits at the table)
We've only had a home of our own for three years and I will
not give it up, not for anyone or anything.

BILL. But if I can't get a job around here —

JOAN. You will. It would be madness to give up this place and
then be unable to find anywhere decent to live wherever a
new job might be. Besides, so far, the salaries offered have
been way beneath what you earned before — and as far as I
can see, we wouldn't be able to afford to live — not at the
standard we're used to.

BILL. There simply aren't any jobs in England in the kind of work
I do. The steel industry is in a bad way, Joan, and not likely
to pick up overnight.

JOAN. *(thinking)* Of course the Social Security money isn't
much —

BILL. And we've used most of our savings.

JOAN. I suppose you could take another temporary job — like

you did over Christmas.

BILL. I could — but I want a permanent job. I can't go on like this.

(There is a depressed pause)

JOAN. Mind you, if something at your old salary was offered — even some distance away — *(She hesitates)*

BILL. *(eagerly)* Yes?

JOAN. I suppose you *could* take a room and come home week-ends —

BILL. You wouldn't mind?

JOAN. Of course I'd mind, but it could be done if the salary was right.

BILL. But no move?

JOAN. Definitely not. Why do you keep asking?

BILL. Well. . . . with the Common market open. . . .

JOAN. Oh, Bill, you wouldn't go rushing off to the Ruhr, would you?

BILL. If I remain out of work, I might go further than that.

JOAN. Don't be so defeatist. Things will come right. If it wasn't for looking after the girls, I'd take a job myself, you know I would. But the girls come first.

BILL. Yes, dear. Of course.

JOAN. The next two or three years are vital to Samantha's future. Her teacher says any change now would be disastrous.

BILL. Surely there are other good schools?

JOAN. Possibly—but not teachers like Miss Hatton. Who knows, Samantha may go to University.

BILL. To University? Whatever for?

JOAN. Really, Bill! I may not be all for Women's Lib. but I don't see why a girl with brains shouldn't have the same educational chance as a boy —

BILL. She'll only get married and drop it all.

JOAN. We don't know that. She must be given her chance.

BILL. I'm sorry, Joan. I'm feeling fed up at the prospect of crawling once more to those types at the Social Security office. They make me feel like something found under a stone.

JOAN. Oh, Bill — I'm sure they're most understanding.

BILL. I don't want sympathy. I want work.

(JOAN gets up, putting a sympathetic hand on his shoulder)

JOAN. Of course you do, dear. I know you're no layabout. . . .
and I care very much about your future.

BILL. Do you?

JOAN. Of course I do. That's why I won't have you take a job
that's beneath you.

BILL. Anything rather than being bloody redundant.

JOAN. Don't let it get you down, Bill. . . . and do remember
the girls.

BILL. The girls?

JOAN. *(gently chiding)* You've been swearing far too freely
lately. It's bound to have a bad effect on them.

BILL. Oh. . . all right.

JOAN. And always remember that *I* don't blame you in any
way for what's happened.

BILL. *(dryly)* Thanks.

JOAN. Though some people may.

BILL. Your mother, for instance?

JOAN. Now, Bill. Please don't start on mother. That reminds me,
she's coming to tea.

BILL. I may be out.

JOAN. Now, dear — you were out last time she came.

BILL. Don't say she missed me!

JOAN. It looks so pointed.

BILL. Some of the things she says are as well.

JOAN. I'll speak to her. People are funny. . . . even Delia.

BILL. *(surprised)* Delia! I thought she understood.

JOAN. So did I, but only yesterday she asked me in a very odd
way 'hasn't he landed a job *yet?*' If she wasn't my best friend
and a very good neighbour, I'd have been rude to her.

BILL. *(put out)* It's not like her. Though, come to think of it,
she did ask me why I hadn't taken the Southampton job.

JOAN. *(quickly)* What did you say?

BILL. That you didn't like the idea of moving.

JOAN. Now, Bill, that's not the entire truth, is it?

BILL & JOAN. *(together)* There's the girls' education —
*(They both stop. Rather annoyed, JOAN crosses to the settee
and plumps up the cushions)*

JOAN. We *must* consider the girls' education. . . . . not to
mention the very doubtful wisdom of leaving a good home.
There *is* a housing shortage, you know.
*(BILL opens his mouth to speak. JOAN holds up a hand and
continues)*

JOAN. You were going to remind me that a house was offered
with the Southampton job — but it was only rented.

BILL. We could have gone to see it.

JOAN. *(banging the cushions)* Besides, it was only a Tool-maker's
job. You're a Charge Hand and used to be proud of it.

BILL. I'm beyond pride.

JOAN. And having to pay rent on the house would have meant
real hardship for all of us — a lowering of our standard of
living.

BILL. We've had to lower it this last year.

JOAN. Only temporarily.

BILL. I could have taken a room in Southampton.

JOAN. Bill! Haven't I just explained it could not be done on the
salary. You're being very difficult this morning.
(There is a silence. JOAN crosses to the kitchen area again)

JOAN. If you weren't so selfish, you'd realise how I feel about
our life here. I and the girls have friends, neighbours,
relatives. We belong. You shouldn't *expect* us to want to
start all over again somewhere else. . . . but then, you're a
man who doesn't seem to need friends.

BILL. I've plenty of friends.

JOAN. *Pub* friends! You're so ashamed of them, you daren't ask
them home.

BILL. *(low)* Not more than once.

JOAN. *(sharply)* What was that?

BILL. Er — I asked what was for lunch.

JOAN. I don't know till I've been to the shops. I must make a

list. And don't try to change the subject. . . . What was I
saying? Oh, yes, about friends. I've always had lots of friends.
Now there's Delia. Since her husband died she utterly depends
on me. We've become very close. I'd hate to leave her. In
fact, I don't know what she'd do without me.

BILL. She's a very nice person, but you could make new friends.

JOAN. I like the ones I have.

*(JOAN takes pad and pencil from a drawer, opens cupboard
and starts to make a list. There is a brief pause)*

BILL. Joan —

JOAN. *(absently)* Yes, dear?

BILL. Just suppose for a moment that a really well paid job
was offered to me —

JOAN. It will be one day.

BILL. No — now. . . but it was some distance away — would
you still refuse to move?

JOAN. I've told you.

BILL. But what would I do? Turn it down?

JOAN. Not necessarily. Didn't I just say that you could take a
room and come home week-ends. . . . .

BILL. But —

JOAN. *(going on)* Though, mind you, I'm against breaking up the
family. . . and there's always the risk of some designing woman
getting hold of you. *(looks at him)* You're at the dangerous age.

BILL. Am I?

JOAN. The mid forties. But there, it's not likely to happen, is it?
(JOAN looks in the "frig" and makes some notes)

BILL. *(persisting)* You wouldn't move — not even to save me
from some designing female?

JOAN. *(leaning over the bar, smiling)* No, dear, I trust you
completely.
*(BILL smiles feebly then as JOAN finishes her list and comes
round the counter, he looks very depressed)*

JOAN. *(checking her money in her handbag)* Now, I'm going to
the shops. The supermarket gets so crowded if I leave it any
later. Besides, I need time to look around and get the best

price. I do help all I can, Bill.

BILL. *(wearily)* I know. I know.

JOAN. Why don't you do some digging? Good for the figure. . .
I think I'll take my mac. It looks as if it might rain. . . . . .
*(JOAN exits to the hall. BILL slips his hand inside his
jacket and looks at a paper he takes out. Then he looks up,
thinking deeply. He sighs. Hearing JOAN come in he quickly
returns the paper to his pocket.*
*JOAN is tying on a headscarf and has a mac over her arm.
She crosses to kitchen area)*

JOAN. I'll take the shopper. Shan't be more than an hour.
*(JOAN brings shopper from behind side door and opens the
door. She looks back, smiling)*

JOAN. I wonder if I might find the dishes done when I get back?
(She exits)
*(Having given his wife a smile of doubtful sincerity, BILL
turns to the window and peers out cautiously. Satisfied that
she has gone, he takes more papers from his pocket and
spreads them on the table. As he studies them intently he
hears a sound. The back door opens He hurriedly scoops up
the papers and stuffs them back into his pocket. DELIA
JONES comes into the kitchen area looking around. She is
a very attractive widow in her late thirties, amusing and
somewhat cynical)*

DELIA. Bill?

BILL. *(rising and coming forward)* Hello there.

DELIA. Is Joan out?

BILL. Yes. You've just missed her.

DELIA. I thought I saw her pass but wasn't sure.

BILL. Do you want to speak to her?

DELIA. It can wait. *(Comes forward)* How are you today?

BILL. Me? Oh, all right, I suppose.
(DELIA comes right down towards the settee)

DELIA. It must be rotten for you, Bill. I'm so very sorry for
you.

BILL. *(eagerly)* Are you?

DELIA. A man out of work — even when it's no fault of his own — is a man with no place in the world.

BILL. *(Pleased)* I thought you blamed me. Joan said —

DELIA. Then Joan misunderstood me. I'm truly sorry for you, Bill.

BILL. It is pretty awful.

DELIA. Bet you feel lost.

BILL. I do.

DELIA. And Joan — without meaning to, of course — makes you feel you're under her feet all the time?

BILL. *(loyally)* She's very patient.

DELIA. And shows it. *(smiles)* Don't we all?

BILL. How understanding you are, Delia. You see, I'm no good in the house. I feel a complete write off.

DELIA. We can't have that.

BILL. We've got it. That's the position, isn't it? I'm redundant. Unwanted.

(There is a short pause)

DELIA. Tell me, Bill — did you really turn down the Southampton job because Joan wouldn't move?

BILL. *(loyal again)* There were other reasons. The low pay for one. Losing our home for another.

DELIA. But there was a house, wasn't there?

BILL. Rented. . . . and there was the girls' schooling to consider. Moving schools isn't a good idea when they are both coming up to exams.

DELIA. That's what Joan thinks?

BILL. And Samantha's teacher.

DELIA. Lots of children have survived it.

BILL. Still, if it isn't essential. . . . .

DELIA. But it is — for you.

BILL. Me? *(He stares at her)*

DELIA. Bill, don't you ever think of yourself?

BILL. *(embarrassed)* Of course. Who doesn't? But I must consider my family too.

DELIA. I sometimes wonder if you're a man or a mouse?

BILL. *(startled)* What?. . . . Good grief, is that how you think of me?

DELIA. Only sometimes. Like now.

BILL. But what can I do? I hate rows, upheavals, all that.

DELIA. There speaks the mouse. Sooner or later you'll have to assert yourself — claim your right to do what suits *you.*

BILL. But Sammy — her teacher says she's got great prospects — educationally speaking.

DELIA. Then it won't matter *where* she is. It's *what* she is.

BILL. And Viki — it would break her heart to be separated from Chris.

DELIA. England is not very big. Travel is fast.

BILL. *(vaguely)* Oh, England. . . . . *(covering up)* No, as you say.

DELIA. As for Joan, she needs a damn good shake-up. She puts her home before all of you.

BILL. I thought you were on her side.

DELIA. You thought wrong.

BILL. But you're her closest friend.

DELIA. Why do you let her make the decisions, Bill? Hasn't Mr. Mouse a mind of his own?

BILL. Yes, of course. . . . . but Joan has always known best.

DELIA. She's got her priorities wrong this time. You should have taken that Southampton job, moved out yourself and let her come to her senses.

BILL. You don't mean that.

DELIA. I do. She would have come running.

(BILL stares at her, his hand straying to his jacket pocket. He starts to speak then stops)

DELIA. What's the matter? You look as if you're about to propose?

BILL. *(his mind elsewhere)* Propose?

DELIA. To me — marriage. *(kidding)* This is so sudden, Bill — though truth to tell, I seem to have been waiting a long while.

BILL. *(aghast)* But — but I didn't mean. . . .

DELIA. You do rise beautifully, Bill!

BILL. Rise? *(realises)* Oh, Delia! What a leg-puller you are.

DELIA. One must do something to get a laugh. Come on what were you going to say?

BILL. Nothing.

DELIA. Out with it! You can't fool me.

BILL. I don't know if –

DELIA. – if you can trust me?

BILL. I didn't mean that, really.

DELIA. You want my advice about something.

BILL. How on earth did you know that?

DELIA. It's my sixth sense.

BILL. Now you're pulling my leg again.

DELIA. Not at all. *(She sits on settee)* Come on – sit here and tell me all about it.

BILL. You won't tell anyone?

DELIA. Cut my throat and hope to die, whatever the jargon is. . . satisfied?

(BILL laughs, sits on settee and eagerly draws out the wad of papers. He selects a single sheet and hands it to DELIA)

DELIA. *(scanning it)* A letter. My, my – from Australia *(Reads and gets excited)* But Bill, this is a simply fabulous offer!

BILL. Think so?

DELIA. *(reading from letter)* 'Selected out of over a hundred applications. . . . . references highly satisfactory' *(She looks up)* And they give you three weeks to decide. My dear Bill, congratulations! You're not a mouse after all!

BILL. *(getting up nervously)* I haven't accepted.

DELIA. But you will?

BILL. I don't know.

DELIA. *(amazed)* You don't know!

BILL. Be reasonable, Delia –

DELIA. Reasonable? When you're being utterly unreasonable?

BILL. But Joan – if she won't move to Southampton, is she likely to move to Australia?

DELIA. *(getting up excitedly)* I told you – go alone. She'll follow.

BILL. But will she? There's the girls' schooling, you see.

DELIA. The New South Wales schools are first class. Remember,
I was out there before I married and I'm in constant touch
with my cousins who live there. I tell you, the girls would not
only find a good school but would have an exciting and healthy
outdoor life too.

BILL. What about housing? They have a worse problem than we
have — haven't they?

DELIA. Only in the cities. You can live outside Newcastle — there
are plenty of pleasant little towns nearby. I think I can help
you about accomodation.

BILL. You can?

DELIA. One of my cousins is in the estate business in Sydney.
I can put you in touch.

BILL. That would be a great help — if I go.

DELIA. As a matter of fact, I was thinking of taking a holiday in
Australia myself. . . . . . later on.

BILL. *(eagerly)* Were you? I say, *that* might influence Joan. . . . I
mean, if she thought you would be near her for a while.

DELIA. It might — and then again, it might not.

BILL. What do you mean? You're her closest friend.

DELIA. Physically speaking — I am.

BILL. Physically? *(laughs)* Oh, being next door! That's a funny
way of putting it.

DELIA. Anyway, you'll tell Joan about this offer?

BILL. You really think I ought to?

DELIA. If you don't, you're Mr. Mouse forever. . . .

BILL. I'm sure she won't take it seriously.

DELIA. That doesn't matter — as long as *you* take it seriously.

BILL. I'm not sure that I do.

DELIA. *(squeaking like a mouse)* Eek!

BILL. *(laughs)* But what about the girls? Won't they hate me for
uprooting them?

DELIA. Once they settle down they'll bless you. Young people
have a wonderful time out there — swimming, sailing, tennis,
dancing all the year round. The Australians know how to
enjoy life.

(There is another slight pause. BILL seems to make up his mind)

BILL. Very well. I'll ask Joan how she feels about it

DELIA. No.

BILL. But you said —

DELIA. Don't ask her — *tell* her.

BILL. Tell her!

DELIA. Yes. Give her the letter and say you've already accepted.

BILL. But I haven't.

DELIA. Then do it now.

BILL. Now?

DELIA. Note paper, envelope, pen.

BILL. *(excited)* Delia — you're a tonic.

DELIA. No. Just another bossy woman. You can't do without them, can you?

(Laughing BILL finds paper and envelope in a drawer and brings them to the table. He sits, taking a pen from his pocket)

BILL. I'll have to think.

(DELIA takes a chair close to BILL. She picks up the other papers BILL has put on the table)

DELIA. What are these?

BILL. From Australia House. It seems the family can get an assisted passage if I've got a job to go to. . . . Now, how shall I start?

DELIA. Make it short. They only want your acceptance. *(looks at letter)* They say details will be sent later.

BILL. Right. *(starts writing)* Dear Sir. . . . . *(stops)*

DELIA. *(continuing for him)* 'Thank you for your letter of the 18th inst. offering me the post of Charge Hand Tool-maker at a salary of 1800 dollars a year'. . . . . . That's more than you were getting here, Bill, isn't it?

BILL. Half as much again. . . . . but then things are more expensive over there, I've been told.

DELIA. Not all that more expensive. It's a very good salary. Go on.

(DELIA looks over his shoulder as he writes)

DELIA. I think I'll type it out for you. Did you have to apply
in writing?

BILL. Only on the questionnaire. I got the letter typed.

DELIA. I'll do it for you.

BILL. Of course, you were a secretary before you married,
weren't you?

DELIA. Yes. Now read out what you've written.

BILL. *(reading)* 'When I have further details I will make all
necessary arrangements to travel in time to start with the
firm on May 1st. *(looks at* DELIA *who holds the original
letter)* That is the right date, isn't it?

DELIA. *(checking)* That's right.

BILL. Ought I to say something about bringing the family with me
— or not? After all, I don't know yet, do I?

DELIA. No, that's not their business. They only want to know
about you.

BILL. Then I'll sign. . . . no, of course not. Will you bring the
typed letter to me, Delia?

DELIA. *(taking draft)* No. Sign at the foot of this page and I'll
fit the letter in and post it off before you change your
mind!

BILL. *(signing his name)* How sure you are, Delia. I've never
been able to make up my mind about major things.

DELIA. I suppose Joan asked you to marry her?

BILL. *(indignantly)* Of course not. . . . . well, in a way, I suppose
she did.

DELIA. Cheer up. Most women do.

BILL. *(surprised)* What — propose?

DELIA. Sort of. Now, you promise to tell Joan today?

BILL. *(uneasily)* I wonder how she'll take it?

DELIA. It doesn't matter. The acceptance will have been posted.

BILL. Yes, so it will. *(rises and puts hand in pocket)* What's the
Air Mail postage?

DELIA. *(rising)* Ninepence.

    *(DELIA comes down stage and BILL joins her, pressing the
coins into her palm. Then he covers her hand with both his)*

BILL. I never knew till now how marvellous you are, Delia.
  (Gratefully BILL *leans forward and kisses* DELIA *on the
  cheek.* DELIA *smiles and turns her lips to his. They kiss.
  The side door opens and an elderly woman,* MRS. PASMORE,
  *comes in, dressed in hat and coat, and carrying a shopping
  bag. She looks outraged. The two spring apart.)*
BILL. *(weakly)* Hello, mother-in-law. . . . . I'm afraid Joan's out.

CURTAIN.

The same afternoon about 4.30 p.m.
MRS PASMORE is just seating herself on the setteee. She takes
a piece of knitting from a bag and settles herself, bolt upright
BILL is seated at the table, reading the afternoon paper.
JOAN is in the kitchen area mixing a salad on the counter in a
large bowl. MRS. PASMORE has just been given a cup of tea.
The other two have had their's and the used cups and saucers
are close by them)

MRS PASMORE. *(Picking up her cup)* You shouldn't have
    bothered dear, so near tea time. But I confess I'm parched after
    that film show.
JOAN. I'm sorry I missed you this morning, Mum. I could have
    done with your opinion about some very cheap shoes. I didn't
    buy them because I wasn't sure they looked all right — and we
    have to be so careful how we spend our money these days.
MRS PASMORE. Cheap shoes don't wear.
    (BILL appears to hear something outside the window. He looks
    agitated, half gets up and sits down again)
JOAN. True enough. What did you and Mrs Bagshaw think of the
    film?
MRS PASMORE. We both thought it was awful.
    (There is a tap at the kitchen door. It is pushed open and
    DELIA comes in. She hesitated at the sight of MRS PASMORE
    and a look passes between her and BILL)
JOAN. *(delighted)* Delia! How nice! I hear I missed you also this
    morning.
DELIA. Also?. . . . . Oh, Mrs Pasmore, of course.
JOAN. Yes. Won't you stay to tea?
    (MRS PASMORE clears her throat loudly, looking at JOAN,
    who takes no notice)
DELIA. Should I? *(She looks from MRS PASMORE to BILL)*
JOAN. Of course you should. It's only cold, but there's plenty.

DELIA. Then I will. Thank you.

JOAN. Good.

DELIA. I dropped in to ask if you felt like coming with me to see the film at the Rialto. They say it's very good.

JOAN. Mum was just going to tell us what she and Mrs Bagshaw thought of it.

DELIA. H'm. . . . that should be interesting.

MRS PASMORE. It's billed as a love story. If that's love, I'm a sex maniac.

DELIA. Oh, I wouldn't say that, Mrs Pasmore.

(MRS PASMORE *looks furious.* JOAN *laughs and* BILL *feels able to join in*)

MRS PASMORE. *(stiffly)* I don't think that remark was at all funny.

JOAN. *(straightening her face)* Sorry, Mum. Delia always makes me laugh.

DELIA. No offence, Mrs Pasmore. You're certainly no maniac. I'm not so sure about the sex.

MRS PASMORE. *I* never went in for seducing other women's husbands.

(BILL *and* DELIA *exchange quick glances.* JOAN *frowns*)

JOAN. Is that what it's about? How dreary. So old-fashioned.

DELIA. I fancy there's more to it than that. Shall I make the salad dressing, Joan?

JOAN. Will you, dear? Bill, pass Delia your cup over the counter, please.

(BILL *gets up and puts his cup and saucer on the counter.* DELIA *takes it*)

DELIA. *(low)* Have you told her?

BILL. *(low)* No.

DELIA. *(aloud)* Thanks, Bill.

(DELIA *takes the cup to the sink. The front door is heard to open and shut. During the following scene* DELIA *gets out oil and vinegar and mixes a salad dressing on the counter, using condiments from a cruet that stands on the counter.*)

JOAN. That'll be Viki.

(VIKI enters with CHRIS. They both look very happy)

JOAN. And Chris! Hello, Chris.

(CHRIS raises a hand in greeting and stands beaming while VIKI salutes her grandmother)

VIKI. Hello, Gran! Hi, Delia. *(looks at her grandmother's knitting)* Is that for me?

MRS PASMORE. No. For your mother.

VIKI. Aren't you kind, Gran? We dress almost entirely in your knitting. . . . . which reminds me I need a new bikini for the summer. Could you knit one for me, Gran? They're so expensive.

MRS PASMORE. I don't think I could.

BILL. Hello, Chris.

CHRIS. Hi, there.

JOAN. Won't you stop to tea, Chris?

CHRIS. Well, no thank you. Mum is expecting me home. I just came to —

VIKI. Dad, we want to go on a hiking holiday at Easter. Chris has got a week's leave. Is that O.K.?

BILL. Sounds a good idea if the weather is O.K.

JOAN. How many of you are going, dear?

VIKI. Just the two of us.

(MRS PASMORE puts down her knitting and looks fixedly at JOAN)

BILL. *(looking at JOAN)* Just the two of you?

VIKI. Yes. We'll stay at Youth Hostels, of course. It'll be ever so cheap.

JOAN. Let's talk it over after tea, shall we?

VIKI. But Chris wants to know, don't you, Chris?

CHRIS. I do, really, Mrs Tennant. I'm going to see the Youth Hostel people tomorrow morning — pay our subscription and make a booking. They get ever so full at Easter and we're a bit late as it is.

BILL. I can't see why they shouldn't

JOAN. If it turns out wet you'll both get your death of cold. . . .

BILL. *(weakly)* Not walking, surely?

MRS PASMORE. I've heard some of those hostels are crawling with vermin.

DELIA. You're thinking of Doss houses, Mrs Pasmore.

MRS PASMORE. I am not thinking of Doss houses. I wouldn't dream of thinking of anything so degrading.

CHRIS. We take our own sleeping bags, so we should be O.K.

VIKI. Don't worry, Gran. I promise not to come back and give you lice — or worse.

MRS PASMORE. *(shuddering)* There is nothing worse.

CHRIS. *(with relish)* Oh, yes there is, Mrs Pasmore. There's plague, scurvy, impetigo — and how about the three Reas?

MRS PASMORE. I've never heard of them.

CHRIS. Pyorrhea, Diahorrhea and gona —

JOAN. *(sharply)* Chris!

CHRIS. Sorry, Mrs Tennant. My brother's joke.

JOAN. *(quickly)* He's a doctor, Mum.

VIKI. Anyway, Chris hasn't got it, so I'm all right.
(All the adults, except DELIA , are startled, but neither of the young people see the implication. VIKI goes to her father and puts an arm around him.)

VIKI. We can go, can't we?

BILL. *(swallowing)* It's for your mother to say.

JOAN. *(hurriedly)* We'll discuss it later.

VIKI. *(leaving go of her father)* But, Mum —

JOAN. That's enough, Viki. Chris, can you come back this evening — or perhaps you could 'phone?

CHRIS. Of course, Mrs Tennant. . . . . *(backing out)* Well, so long. . . . .
(VIKI, annoyed, goes with CHRIS. There is a brief silence broken by DELIA)

DELIA. Can I set the table for you, Joan?

JOAN. *(distracted)* The table? Oh, yes, please Delia. *(dithering)* I wonder where Samantha is? She's late.
(DELIA comes round the counter, takes cutlery etc. from a drawer and begins to lay the table)

MRS PASMORE. If I were you, I would not let her go away with that boy.

BILL. Nonsense. Chris is a very nice chap.

MRS PASMORE. Telling jokes like that isn't my idea of a nice
   boy.

BILL. It's a common medical student joke.

MRS PASMORE. Common is the word. . . . and I can only hope
   Victoria's remark was an innocent one.

DELIA. You have doubts, Mrs Pasmore?

BILL. *(to* DELIA*)* What a filthy mind!

JOAN. *(to* DELIA*)* Of course Gran has no doubts about our girls.
   We do not belong to the permissive society.

MRS PASMORE. Speak for yourself Joan.

BILL. *(getting up angry)* The girls are all right. I won t hear
   anything against them. They're all right.

MRS PASMORE. *(distinctly)* Small thanks to their father.
   *(*BILL *turns away abruptly, glancing at* DELIA *who is quite
   unperturbed.* JOAN *comes down towards her mother)*

JOAN. Now, Mum, I think that was uncalled for

MRS. PASMORE. None so blind. . . . . .

JOAN. *(obviously referring to what she has been told)* Really.
   Mum, let's hear no more about *that*, please.

MRS PASMORE. As you wish.

JOAN. And don't think we are not aware of the faults in our
   children. They have faults — so have we. We are all human

DELIA. *(dryly)* Some less than others.

JOAN. *(pretending to ignore this)* But they are not immoral—
   and I don't think you have any reason to suggest they are.

MRS PASMORE. I never said such a thing.

BILL. You hinted at it.

MRS PASMORE. *(ignoring him)* Well. . . . don't say I didn't
   warn you, Joan.

JOAN. I won't.

DELIA. *(coming forward)* Warn you about what, Joan?

JOAN. Oh, nothing. One of Mum's flights of imagination.

MRS. PASMORE. Imagination!

   *(*DELIA *moves to an arm chair and sits while* BILL *hovers*

nervously behind her)

DELIA. *(laughing)* I do believe you thought Bill was kissing me
   when you came in this morning, Mrs Pasmore!

MRS PASMORE. I believe what I saw.

DELIA. *(to JOAN)* He was taking an eyelash out of my eye.

MRS PASMORE. So you said at the time.

JOAN. Mum, please — remember Delia is my best friend.

MRS PASMORE. Really?

   *(The front door opens and shuts with a bang. SAMANTHA is
   heard calling excitedly)*

SAMANTHA. *(off)* Mum! Dad!

JOAN. Here, darling.

   (SAMANTHA bounds in, followed by VIKI)

VIKI. What's all the noise about, Sammy?

JOAN. Calm down, Samantha dear.

   *(SAMANTHA has been twirling around, humming some sort
   of victory tune to herself)*

BILL. What's up, Sammy?

SAMANTHA. *(coming to rest)* Mum — Dad — Gran — what d'you
   think?

BILL. Good news?

SAMANTHA. Right. Guess what?

BILL. You've floored Harry for good?

SAMANTHA. No, silly. Something important. Guess, Mum.

JOAN. I can't Samantha. Do tell us.

VIKI. Go on, Sammy *(to the others)* Bet it's nothing.

SAMANTHA. You have a go, Gran.

   (SAMANTHA flings herself on to the settee)

MRS PASMORE. Now you've made me drop a stitch.

DELIA. *(rising and coming back to the table)* You're the new
   leader of Woman's Lib.

SAMANTHA. No, it's something far more exciting than that.

JOAN. Good heavens — it must be world shaking!

SAMANTHA. No one can guess? *(She looks round)*

BILL. Do go on. The suspense is killing us.

SAMANTHA. The Head told me I was to take 'A' levels this year.

VIKI. *This year!* But I'm only taking 'O' levels this year.

SAMANTHA. *(showing off)* We can't all be the Brain of Britain.

JOAN. Darling, it's absolutely splendid!

MRS PASMORE. Personally I don't approve of the child being
    pushed like this.

BILL. For once I agree with you mother-in-law.

SAMANTHA. Oh, Dad! But you haven't heard it all yet. Mr.
    Sangster said I could then do a year's further education and,
    if I wished, go on to Teacher Training College. What do you
    think of that?

MRS PASMORE. It's a good idea, but I still can't see why there's
    any hurry.

VIKI. She may not get her 'A' levels this year.

JOAN. Of course she will — if she wants to. I think we should
    be very pleased that the school take such an interest in
    Samantha.

BILL. She'll keep the children in order, anyway. Any trouble
    and POW — they're knocked out.
    (They all laugh except MRS PASMORE)

SAMANTHA. We talked about that — Mr. Sangster and me — and
    I told him I didn't fancy teaching children, so I'll train to
    teach teachers.

VIKI. *(jealous)* Get me!

DELIA. Congrats, Sammy. But don't be in too much of a hurry.

JOAN. Didn't I tell you, Bill that Samantha's education was
    important? And you talking about changing schools and
    ruining her chances.

SAMANTHA. *(leaping up, dismayed)* Changing schools! But
    why? I just couldn't ! I wouldn't do it!

JOAN. Don't worry, darling. You won't have to — I promise.
    (BILL exchanges a glance with DELIA. He looks glum)

MRS PASMORE. Don't you work to hard, Samantha. Next
    year will do just as well. Why you'll not be quite seventeen
    then. It's ridiculous to expect so much of you.

JOAN. Not at all. Learning comes easy to our youngest.

DELIA. *(coming forward)* I'm sure Sammy will do well,

whenever she takes her exam. . . . . but I suggest that when it comes to further education, or a Teacher Training College, it might be a very good idea to go abroad.

SAMANTHA. Abroad?

JOAN. What *are* you saying, Delia?

DELIA. Travelling abroad widens the outlook. Don't you agree, Bill?

BILL. Er — as a matter of fact, yes. It might be just the job.

SAMANTHA. But I don't want to go abroad.

JOAN. Nor you shall, darling. *(to BILL)* I wouldn't dream of sending our baby among foreigners.

DELIA. She'd hardly be a baby by then.

JOAN. I'm surprised at you, Delia. Its the silliest idea I've ever heard.

MRS PASMORE. Just what one might expect from you, Delia Jones.

BILL. *(roused)* I think it's a very good idea.

SAMANTHA. I don't. *(quoting)* The English education is the best in the world, my teacher says. Besides, I've got all my friends here.

DELIA. Pity. You could join your father, Sammy.

(BILL looks thoroughly scared as everyone looks at him)

JOAN. Join *Bill?*

DELIA. *(coolly)* Yes. Tell them, Bill.

JOAN. What in the world are you talking about, Delia?

DELIA. It's for Bill to tell you, Joan dear, More good news?

JOAN. Good news? What?

BILL. Well. . . . . . I've been offered — *(DELIA nudges him)* er. . . I've accepted a job.

SAMANTHA. Good old Dad!

BILL. Better pay than I've ever had — work right up my street — starting May 1st.

(There is a general exclamation of delight and the two girls hurl themselves at their father and embrace him)

VIKI. Congrats Dad!

SAMANTHA. I always knew you'd do it!

MRS PASMORE. *(tartly)* About time too.

JOAN. *(coming forward)* Just a moment. . . . .
    (They all turn to look at her)

JOAN. Delia, you were speaking about Samantha joining Bill
    abroad. . . . . d'you mean you've accepted a job in one of the
    Common Market countries, Bill?

BILL. Of course not, I can't speak any of their lingo.

JOAN. So where is this job?

VIKI. I know — Ireland!

BILL. Further than that, I'm afraid.

JOAN. I suppose this means we only see you week-ends?

SAMANTHA. Oh, no, Dad!

BILL. *(nervously)* I'm afraid even week-ends will be — er —
    difficult.

JOAN. Difficult?

SAMANTHA. What do you mean, Dad?

JOAN. Where *is* this job for heaven's sake?

BILL. *(swallowing hard)* Australia.

CURTAIN.

SCENE 3

About 4.30 p.m. a week later
(SAMANTHA is sitting in an arm chair with a book open, her case on the floor, open. She keeps looking towards the door. The front door is heard to open and bang shut. VIKI comes in carrying a case and a couple of books under her arm)

SAMANTHA. Oh, good. I've been waiting for you, Viki. What did you think of the film?
VIKI. *(lowering her voice and looking around)* Where are the parents?
(VIKI drops her case and books by the other arm chair and starts to take off her blazer)
SAMANTHA. In the garden.
(VIKI crosses towards window up L.)
VIKI. *(amused)* Yes, I see. Dad is digging as if — as if he's trying to get through to Australia.
SAMANTHA. *(laughs)* It may be his only hope!
(VIKI returns to arm chair, flinging her blazer on top of her case)
VIKI. And Mum is pruning like a lady. *(She sits)* Are they speaking?
SAMANTHA. I don't think so. Viki — I've been dying to discuss the film with you. What did you think of it?
VIKI. *(settling snugly into the arm chair)* Well, it may be called sex education but it didn't teach me anything.
SAMANTHA. *(without conviction)* Nor me. *(Pause)* You know, I don't think I'd like a camera looking up me like that.
VIKI. I wouldn't mind if it was only a camera. . . . .
SAMANTHA. Oh. . . . . yes. Wonder what the photographer thought?
VIKI. Just a job, I suppose.
SAMANTHA. And I wonder what the boys thought?

VIKI. They asked a lot of questions.

SAMANTHA. Yes. *(Pause)* The girls didn't did they?

VIKI. No. . . . . Well, the boys asked them all.

SAMANTHA. Yes.

(There is another short pause)

SAMANTHA. *(thinking)* I was a bit disappointed about *how* you do it.

VIKI. How?

SAMANTHA. I mean there they were, just one on top of another — is that all?

VIKI. *(with lofty scorn)* It wasn't supposed to be a film on the eighty-seven positions, you know.

SAMANTHA. *(astounded) Are* there eighty-seven positions?

VIKI. Something like that. I read it somewhere.

SAMANTHA. Now, *that's* interesting!

(There is a pause in which SAMANTHA arranges her hands in possible positions)

VIKI. What *are* you doing?

SAMANTHA. I can't think of more than three — can you?

VIKI. I haven't thought about it at all.

SAMANTHA. Oh, don't be so — Victorian.

VIKI. As a matter of fact, I was wondering if I agree about it being natural to have sexual relations as soon as you want to.

SAMANTHA. Why not?

VIKI. Well. . . . Chris doesn't like the idea.

SAMANTHA. How d'you know?

VIKI. I know him pretty well and he doesn't like the idea of promiscuity at all.

SAMANTHA. He's actually said so?

VIKI. Not *said* so. I just know.

SAMANTHA. You mean you've tried to seduce him?

VIKI. Sammy!

SAMANTHA. You have.

VIKI. I haven't!

SAMANTHA. Go on — admit it.

VIKI. Well. . . . in a way. After all, one *has* feelings.

SAMANTHA. You can always get rid of them yourself.

VIKI. Sammy! *(Pause)* Do you?

SAMANTHA. Of course — sometimes. . . . and the film said it was O.K. That part was good.

VIKI. I don't know. It's all right for a boy, of course. . . . .

SAMANTHA. Why should it be all right for a boy and not for a girl?

VIKI. Well. . . . you know. . . . they've got it there. . . . I mean . . . sort of getting in the way. . . . .

SAMANTHA. The feeling's the same.

VIKI. How do we know?

SAMANTHA. *(getting on to her soap box)* Of course it is. It makes me mad all this 'one thing for boys and another for girls'. It's an imposition of old social values. Thank goodness they're changing. . . .

VIKI. *(teasing)* The girls or the boys?

SAMANTHA. The social values, of course. Just because I've grown into what's called a woman I'm not going to give up my right to have as much fun, have as many adventures and as much freedom as any man — all my life.

VIKI. You'll feel different when you fall in love and have babies.

SAMANTHA. I shan't.

VIKI. You will.

SAMANTHA. I won't

VIKI. *I* did.

SAMATHA. You're Viki — Victorian — A Victorian Miss!

VIKI. Not at all. I'm every bit as progressive as you are. I *did* try to seduce Chris.

SAMANTHA. *(jeering)* Well! That's not progressive — that's really Victorian. Girls and boys don't seduce each other now — they make love because they feel like it, when they feel like it. Seduction is out!

VIKI. Oh, you're impossible! There's no arguing with you. *(There is an offending silence. But SAMANTHA is deep in thought again)*

SAMANTHA. I wonder how many positions *she* knows?

VIKI. Who?

SAMANTHA. Delia. She's what I call sophisticated. I wouldn't mind being like her.

VIKI. Bet *she* believes in seduction.

SAMANTHA. Funny her being such a friend of Mum's . . . . *(has a new thought)* And what about Mum and Dad? How about them? Bet they don't know many.

VIKI. You really are awful. One doesn't discuss one's parents in such a — *(stops)*

SAMANTHA. *(grinning)* position?

VIKI. Situation.

SAMANTHA. Same thing. I bet they only know the one.
    (VIKI tries to maintain a severe look in the face of SAMANTHA's mischievous grin. She can't They both burst out laughing)

VIKI. With Mum on top!
    (They collapse into helpless giggles. Suddenly the side door opens and JOAN comes in from the garden, wearing a macintosh and heavy shoes)

SAMANTHA. Ssh!
    (The girls smother their mirth and pretend to be busy with their books)

JOAN. *(leaning over the counter)* Oh, you're both back. Put the kettle on, Viki dear, while I change my shoes.

VIKI. *(rising)* Yes, Mum.
    (VIKI hurries round the counter and plugs in the kettle, while JOAN. sits and takes off her garden shoes)

JOAN. It's dreadfully muddy in the garden.
    (BILL comes in with mud on his face and on his old mac. JOAN moves her knees round to allow him to get in, then holds up a peremptory hand to stop him going further. She then points down at his feet)

BILL. *(looking down)* Oh, yes. Boots. Where are my slippers?
    (BILL can't reach his slippers without stepping off the mat. VICKI moves to fetch them, but JOAN tugs at her skirt and

stops her. BILL *takes off his wellingtons by dint of standing first on one leg, then on the other. Then he steps off the mat and puts on his slippers.*
VIKI *stands by the kettle, not approving of this performance. The kettle boils)*

VIKI. Kettle boiling, Mum.

JOAN. *(rising)* Thanks dear. I'll take a cup upstairs while I wash and change. Will you have one with me, Viki?

BILL. *(before the word 'Viki' is out)* Yes, please.

VIKI. Oh, no thank you, Mum. I'll wait till tea.
(JOAN has taken a cup and saucer from the cupboard, also tea bags and sugar. She now takes a jug of milk from the "frig". She put all on the counter, unplugs the kettle and pours boiling water into her cup etc.)

SAMANTHA. What's for tea?

JOAN. Fish fingers and chips.

SAMANTHA. Goody.

JOAN. It looks as if it's going to be a good year for roses — heaps of buds. I've done a pretty stiff pruning as I didn't do much last year.
(Nobody seems interested. JOAN picks up her cup of tea and comes round the counter and walks towards the hall door)

JOAN. *(to the air)* Tell your father he can wash in the kitchen.
(She exits)
(VIKI has followed her mother. She looks back at her father grinning)

BILL. *(touching his forelock)* Yes ma'am.
(Both the girls laugh)

SAMANTHA. Dad! You really are awful.

BILL. You shouldn't be talking to me, you know.
(BILL takes another cup and saucer from the cupboard, puts a teabag in the cup and fills it with hot water, adding milk and sugar)

SAMANTHA. It's silly.

VIKI. You'll have to give in to Mum in the end, Dad. You always do.

(BILL turns the tap on in the kitchen and sluices his face over the sink)

SAMANTHA. I'm afraid Viki's right, Dad. And this time I agree with Mum.

VIKI. Me, too. Who wants to go to Australia?

SAMANTHA. Emigrants come back from there in droves.

(BILL dries his face and hands and looks over the counter to SAMANTHA)

BILL. What source of information did you tap for that bit of propaganda, Sammy?

SAMANTHA. Alfred.

BILL. And how would Alfred know?

SAMANTHA. His father's the milkman.

(BILL comes round the counter carrying his cup of tea)

BILL. I begin to understand the true value of the Comprehensive School.

(As BILL crosses to one of the armchairs and sits, there is a knock at the front door. VIKI immediately crosses to the door)

VIKI. That's Chris. I'm expecting him.

(VIKI exits to hall)

VIKI. *(off)* Coming, Chris. *(calling off)* It's only Chris, Mum.

JOAN. *(off, distant)* Right. Give him a cup of tea.

(The front door opens)

VIKI. *(off)* Come in, Chris. . . . .

(Front door closes. VIKI comes in followed by CHRIS, looking rather uncertain)

VIKI. Come and get a cup of tea.

BILL. *(looking up from his paper)* Hi, Chris.

CHRIS. Oh, hello. . . . .

(He hurries after VIKI who has gone into the kitchen area. While VIKI plugs in the kettle and then makes a cup of tea, she and CHRIS talk in low tones)

VIKI. You know what to say?

CHRIS. You've told me often enough.

VIKI. Be firm.

CHRIS. I'll try.

SAMANTHA. What are you two whispering about?

VIKI. Nothing about *you*, nosey. *(low)* Remember, Chris, it's in a good cause.

CHRIS. Rather! but won't he be angry?
    (They both look towards BILL)

VIKI. I hope he will.

CHRIS. Oh. Of course.

VIKI. You're not weakening? This is an attack with a purpose, remember.

CHRIS. I'm not weakening.

VIKI. We've got to make him see he's wrong. Here, *(aloud)* take your tea and go and sit down, Chris.

CHRIS. *(aloud)* Fine. Thanks. *(low, indicating SAMANTHA)* What about her?

VIKI. I'll get her out. And remember to cough when you're ready for me to come in.
    (CHRIS nods. VIKI precedes him and they both come down to BILL)

VIKI. Dad — Chris wants a word with you. *(turning to her sister)* A *private* word, Sammy.

SAMANTHA. Private?

VIKI. Yes. *(She gestures SAMANTHA towards the door)*

SAMANTHA. *(unwillingly)* Oh, all right!
    (SAMANTHA picks up some books and joins VIKI. They both exit)

CHRIS. *(hovering)* Do you mind if I sit here and drink my tea, Mr. Tennant?

BILL. Not at all. Be my guest. You wanted a word?

CHRIS. *(unhappily)* Yes.

BILL. How surprising. No one round here is talking to me.
    (CHRIS grins feebly and sips his tea. BILL waits, paper on his knee)

BILL. Well, what's on your mind?

CHRIS. Well, Mr. Tennant. . . . it's about Viki and me. . . .

BILL. Viki and you? Something gone wrong with the Easter

holiday?

CHRIS. No, not that. Nothing wrong — exactly.

BILL. Nothing wrong?

CHRIS. No, But you see, we love each other.

BILL. You love each other so nothing is wrong. *(jumping to a wrong conclusion)* Good grief, don't tell me!

CHRIS. What?

BILL. Tell her mother — not me.

CHRIS. Oh, but she knows already. She doesn't mind.

BILL. *(aghast)* Doesn't mind? Isn't that carrying permissiveness a bit far?

CHRIS. I don't really know what you're on about.

BILL. *(hoping he is mistaken)* Suppose you tell me.

CHRIS. What I want to talk to you about?

BILL. Yes.

CHRIS. Well — it's quite simple. Viki and I don't want to be separated.

BILL. Separated? *(the truth dawns on him)* Oh, you mean — because of going to Australia?

CHRIS. Of course. What did you think — — ?

BILL. *(hastily)* It doesn't matter. Do go on.

CHRIS. I felt it only right to let you know how we feel. I mean, I simply can't let her go. . . . . if you're really going, that is?

BILL. *If* I'm going?

CHRIS. You mean, you *are* going?

BILL. So far as I know we're all going. Who said we weren't?

CHRIS. Oh, nobody — in particular.

BILL. I thought nobody knew nothing.

CHRIS. What?

BILL. Skip it. You were saying?

CHRIS. *(doggedly)* About Viki and me. . . . .

BILL. About Viki and you?

CHRIS. Yes. She's not going with you.

BILL. I see. What would she do on her own?

CHRIS. Oh, she won't be on her own. I've made plans.

BILL. You have?

CHRIS. She can stay with my parents, then as soon as she's eighteen, we can get married.

BILL. And what do your parents think of the plan?

CHRIS. Well — I haven't told them yet. *(rushing on)* I thought I ought to find out first how *you* felt.

BILL. Very right and proper. *(Pause)* You say you've told Joan?

CHRIS. Viki told her.

BILL. And she doesn't object?

CHRIS. Well. . . not exactly. . . .

BILL. Don't say she left it to me?

CHRIS. Well — not exactly.

BILL. *(thoughtfully)* I see.

CHRIS. *(startled)* You what?

BILL. I see she *has* left it to me. Of course, you realise Viki can't do as she pleases until she is eighteen?

CHRIS. That's in three months.

BILL. So she may have to come out with us to Australia.

CHRIS. You'll force her to go?

BILL. I wouldn't put it like that, Chris. She'll have a nice trip and time to make up her mind whether she wants to come back and marry you or not —

CHRIS. That's what I'm afraid of — the 'not'.

BILL. That's life. It's a gamble.

CHRIS. I — I — *(words fail him)*

(CHRIS looks towards the hall door and seems to have a coughing attack. Much too soon VIKI bounces in, all smiles. CHRIS gives her the thumbs down sign. She immediately looks annoyed, takes his arm and sweeps him towards the kitchen area)

VIKI. I'll pour you another cup of tea, Chris.

CHRIS. I don't think I wa —

VIKI. *(in his ear)* Yes, you do!

(They go into the kitchen area and VIKI plugs in the kettle., SAMANTHA comes in with her books, looking from her father to Chris, try to fathom what has happened. VIKI is whispering urgently to CHRIS)

SAMANTHA. Is it all right to go on with my homework here?
    It's too bloody cold in the bedroom.
BILL. Sammy! You'll get me into trouble.
SAMANTHA. Can t. You're in it already.
    (As SAMANTHA settles at the table JOAN bustles in, having
    changed into a charming frock. BILL's eyebrows go up. JOAN
    looks at VIKI, who shakes her head and brings CHRIS round
    the counter)
CHRIS. Sorry I must go now, Mrs Tennant.
JOAN. Oh, must you, Chris? Give my regards to your parents.
BILL. And mine, too, Chris.
CHRIS. Oh – er – yes.
    (CHRIS exits hastily. VIKI gives her father a baleful look)
VIKI. You'll be sorry for this! (She exits)
JOAN. What was that – –
    (JOAN stops short, remembering she is not speaking to her
    husband. She carries her cup and saucer into the kitchen area.
    SAMANTHA bursting with curiosity, goes to the counter and
    speaks in a low voice)
SAMANTHA. What was that all about?
JOAN. (low) I wouldn't know, dear. (aloud) How was the sex
    education film?
SAMANTHA. Boring. (returns to table and sits) Nothing we didn't
    know.
JOAN. As I expected. I've always tried to be open with you girls
    when you asked questions, unlike your father.
    (BILL pretends not to hear. There is a ring at the front door)
JOAN. (feigning innocence) Now who can that be?
    (There are female voices in the hall. The door opens and VIKI
    comes in with a well-dressed woman in her middle thirties.
    She is MISS HATTON, Samantha's teacher. SAMANTHA
    jumps up all smiles)
VIKI. Mum – it's Miss Hatton. . . . . . .
SAMANTHA. Hello, Miss Hatton. Did you want to talk to me?
MISS HATTON. No, dear – I want a word with your father.
    (JOAN has come forward from the kitchen area, very full of

charm)

JOAN. Why, of course, Miss Hatton. Girls — go into your room and take your books.

SAMANTHA. *(collecting her books, to* VIKI*)* It's like musical chairs this afternoon. . . . what's she want to talk to Dad for?

VIKI. Search me.

(They go out together. BILL has risen, somewhat alarmed. He shakes hands with MISS HATTON)

MISS HATTON. We've met at various school functions I think, Mr. Tennant?

BILL. Yes, yes indeed. Won't you sit down?

MISS HATTON. *(sitting on settee)* Thank you.

JOAN. *(hovering)* You want me to stay, Miss Hatton?

MISS HATTON. Of course. It concerns the girls — Samantha in particular.

JOAN. Can I offer you a cup of tea? The kettle is only just off the boil.

MISS HATTON. No, thank you. I can't stay long.

(JOAN sits on the settee. BILL resumes his chair. There is a slight pause)

JOAN. About the girls you said, Miss Hatton?

MISS HATTON. Yes — particularly Samantha.

BILL. Oh, yes, Sammy. She told us what Mr. Sangster said.

MISS HATTON. She has an unusually keen intelligence. She will go far.

BILL. *(facetiously)* She's going to Australia for a start.

(He starts to laugh, but stops seeing their frozen faces)

MISS HATTON. It was about the Australian proposition that I wished to speak to you, Mr. Tennant.

BILL. It's rather more than a proposition —

JOAN. *(frowning)* Bill!. . . . . Yes, do go on, Miss Hatton.

MISS HATTON. Well, you both know that we hope Samantha will be able to go on to Teacher Training College?

BILL. She told us.

MISS HATTON. The first step is to get her 'A' levels. If she is taken away from school before the examination she will be unable to take the equivalent until next year in Australia.

BILL. At her age that hardly matters.

JOAN. Bill, please. . . . .

MISS HATTON. *(looking severely at* BILL*)* I was about to point out that Samantha would then have to start a totally different study programme, which would certainly upset her chance of doing well.

JOAN. I do so agree with you, Miss Hatton.

MISS HATTON. In my opinion, it's a chance the child should not have to take. Her future *must* be considered.

BILL. *(quietly)* And mine?

JOAN. Now Bill, that's quite irrelevant.

MISS HATTON. Not entirely, Mrs Tennant —

BILL. *(dryly)* Thanks a lot.

MISS HATTON. It really depends *whose* future is the more important, doesn't it? I mean, Mr. Tennant has had a lot of his already. Samantha hasn't.

JOAN. True. True.

*(*BILL*'s face betrays what he thinks of that)*

MRS HATTON. And of course the education over there is nothing like as good as it is here.

JOAN. That goes without saying.

MISS HATTON. It had to be said.

BILL. Had it?

(The two women look at BILL *as if they had not realised he was there)*

JOAN. *(turning back to* MISS HATTON*)* You were saying?

MISS HATTON. Samantha being uprooted at this point in her schooling would, in my opinion, be throwing away a certainty for a hazard.

JOAN. Beautifully put, dear Miss Hatton.

BILL. *(greatly daring)* I have it on good authority that the schools in New South Wales are excellent.

JOAN. Whose authority? Australia House, I suppose? They've got to blow their own trumpet, haven't they?

BILL. No, from someone who has lived there and has many

relations there now.

JOAN. *(to BILL)* You mean Delia? *(to MISS HATTON)* Our neighbour, Delia Jones. But she hasn't been there for twenty years, and of course she's not up in the education world.

MISS HATTON. *I* do speak with some authority.

(BILL is squashed)

JOAN. Of course. We realise that.

MISS HATTON. The very fact of a girl having graduated at an English Teacher Training College is a guarantee of a top grade job anywhere.

JOAN. Goes without saying.

BILL. *(getting in first)* It had to be said.

MISS HATTON. What? *(realising her leg was being pulled. Coldly)* In the circumstances —

BILL. What circumstances?

MISS HATTON. Of your going to Australia. . . . . in the circumstances I suggest you and Mrs Tennant think over the possible results on Samantha very carefully — very carefully indeed.

JOAN. Oh, we will, Miss Hatton. I've told my husband already that I think any move now would be disastrous.

MISS HATTON. Disastrous.

(They both look severely at BILL)

BILL. *(clearing his throat)* Well. . . . what do you suggest, Miss Hatton?

(Thus appealed to, MISS HATTON thaws)

MISS HATTON. It seems to me there are two courses of action open to you, Mr. Tennant.

BILL. Exactly. We go or we stay.

MISS HATTON. *(taken aback)* Er — not exactly. The first course I agree, is to give up the project —

BILL. It's rather more than a project, Miss Hatton. I've accepted the job.

MISS HATTON. You have an excuse — a valid excuse — for changing your mind, Mr. Tennant.

BILL. And if I don't change my mind?

MISS HATTON. I suggest you could leave Samantha here to finish her education.

JOAN. What — for three years?

MISS HATTON. I'm sure accomodation could be found for her with one of the parents.

BILL. Leave her here alone — for all that time?

MISS HATTON. It would be worth it.

(There is a pause)

JOAN. It's a most difficult decision, Miss Hatton. To be separated from one's children for so long would be a great sacrifice.

BILL. Children? Is Viki staying too?

JOAN. She ought to. If she doesn't take her 'O' levels this year she never will.

BILL. In Viki's case, I hardly think it matters.

MISS HATTON. *(outraged)* No 'O' levels? She'd not be able to hold any position in the world at all!

BILL. I doubt she needs 'O' levels to get married — or am I mistaken?

(MISS HATTON is going to reply, but thinks better of it. She rises abruptly. JOAN springs up, glaring at BILL)

MISS HATTON. I really must go.

JOAN. Dear Miss Hatton — thank you so much for taking such a personal interest in the future of our youngest.

MISS HATTON. *(pressing JOAN's hand)* I'll leave you both to talk things over. I'm sure your decision will be the right one. Samantha's future is in your hands. *(Coldly)* Good-bye, Mr. Tennant.

BILL. *(rising slowly)* Good-bye.

(The two women exit)

And good riddance.

(BILL sits. The front door closes. BILL hides behind his newspaper as JOAN enters)

JOAN. *(fuming)* What an exhibition! Now you have shown yourself in your true colours, Bill Tennant.

BILL. Colours? What colours?

JOAN. To think I have been married all these years to a monster
  — a cold-hearted, selfish monster!

BILL. Are you talking about me?

JOAN. Yes, you!

  *(BILL shrugs and raises his newspaper as a shield. JOAN
  snatches it from him and throws it on the settee)*

JOAN. I'll say it again. Monster.

BILL. *(nodding)* Monster.

JOAN. How you could sit there casually agreeing to lose your
  two daughters just to satisfy a whim to dash off to the other side
  of the world —

BILL. *(staggered)* Whim?

JOAN. I've heard about this urge in middle-aged men. They do
  the wildest things, forget all responsibilities, all loyalty, all
  family ties — leave their homes and loves ones, perhaps never
  to see them again. . . . .

BILL. But that isn't the idea at all.

JOAN. *(sweeping on, getting hysterical)* Oh, I never thought *you*
  would do such a thing! What's happened to us? I thought we
  were so close, Bill, cared for all of us. . . . . but you don't care
  for me any longer, or the children! I can't believe it's
  happening. . . . . I can't believe it! *(She sits and starts to weep)*
  *(BILL is completely taken in. He gets up and sits beside her on
  the settee, putting an arm round her)*

BILL. But it's not like that at all, Joan. Of course I still care for
  you and the children. Of course I do!

JOAN. You've a funny way of showing it. Goodness knows I've
  always been a good wife to you, haven't I?

BILL. Of course you have.

JOAN. Then what have I done to deserve this?

BILL. I might as well ask — what have *I* done?

JOAN. *(wrenching herself away)* Don't twist things!

BILL. Me? . . . . I've only accepted a job that will keep us all
  very nicely. What's wrong with that?

JOAN. *(turning on the tears again)* You want to get away from
  us — abandon us — leave your family. . . . .

BILL. *(bewildered)* I'm not abandoning anyone – unless you
 mean Samantha, and it's *you* who wants her to stay and finish
 her education, not me!

JOAN. I refuse to be responsible for ruining my own daughter's
 future!

BILL. Well then, it's not me who is abandoning her.

JOAN. Of course you are. And Viki ought to stay here too –
 especially as she wants to be with Chris. She *shall* stay. If you
 go to Australia you will be abandoning both of them.

BILL. But that's crazy!

JOAN. So I'm crazy now!

BILL. If you think it's best that both girls stay here, we're not
 abandoning them, are we? We'll see they are well cared for,
 find a lovely home for them in Australia and they can join
 us. How about that?
 (JOAN turns on him furiously)

JOAN. Not so fast. *(dramatically)* You don't think *I* could leave
 my children, do you? I can't even if you can. No. If they stay,
 I stay.
 (BILL, goaded, loses his temper)

BILL. All right, then! They don't stay. We all go, just as it should
 be.

JOAN. *(beating at his chest with her fists)* You beast! I'd never
 have a moment's peace knowing I'd ruined Samantha's
 future and broken Viki's heart. You may be a monster, but
 I'm not!

BILL. But Joannie darling, you can't want me to throw such a
 marvellous chance up?

JOAN. Don't you 'Joannie' me! You go on your own or you
 stay here with your family. Choose. Which is it to be?

BILL. *(flummoxed)* I – I don't know. I never thought you
 would –

JOAN. Well, I would and I will. *(Walks to hall door)* I'll stay here
 with the girls unless you come to your senses.

BILL. *(moving after her)* But Joannie – how do I know you –
 or the girls – will ever join me?

JOAN. *(at him)* You don't!

(BILL suddenly loses his temper)

BILL. I've had about enough of this. You're being utterly unreasonable.

JOAN. *I* am! It's you who's being utterly unreasonable and totally selfish!

BILL. Oh, go to — — your mother!

JOAN. That's exactly where I *am* going.

(JOAN exits, slamming the door)

BILL. Damn. Blast. Hell.

(There are excited female voices in the hall. Then the front door slams. The door from the hall opens. SAMANTHA and VIKI stand there accusingly)

SAMANTHA. What have you done to Mum?

VIKI. She's crying.

SAMANTHA. She says she's gone to Gran.

VIKI. You'll be sorry for this!

BILL. *(wearily)* You said that before.

VIKI. Oh! *(She flounces out)*

SAMANTHA. I'm going after Mum.

BILL. All right. All right. Go.

(SAMANTHA exits, slamming the door. BILL winces. He paces up and down distractedly. The front door slams. He winces)

BILL. *(still pacing)* Women! They're all in it together — the whole ruddy lot of them. Whatever I do I'll be in the wrong. I just can't win!

(The side door opens cautiously and DELIA peeps in. She wears a coat but no hat. She steps quietly in and closes the door behind her)

BILL. *(fuming on)* Sammy, Viki, Joan and mother-in-law. . . . . there's no one on *my* side, not one ruddy one. . . . .

(He catches sight of someone at the kitchen door. He turns and sees it is DELIA. She smiles at him. He stares, fascinated. She is like the answer to prayer)

QUICK CURTAIN.

ACT TWO

SCENE 1

The same afternoon, about 15 minutes later.

DELIA *is seated with* BILL *on the settee. She wears a colourful and very short dress which becomes her exceedingly. Her coat is draped across a chair.*
There is a bottle of whisky on the coffee table and two glasses.
DELIA *picks up the bottle.*

BILL. So you see what a dilemma I'm in, Delia.

DELIA. You certainly are. Just a drop more?

BILL. What a pal you are, Delia — to go and fetch this to cheer me up.

DELIA. I'm only sorry I couldn't ask you to my place — but with the builder in looking around and making an estimate. . . . .

BILL. We're alone here for a while, anyway. You're having the place done up?

DELIA. Repairs as well. *(She puts bottle down)* Well, now I know why Joan fled like a bat out of hell, followed by Samantha. I simply had to come in and find out what was going on.

BILL. Am I glad you did! I was in the vilest temper and you've calmed me down no end, though, mind you, I'm still pretty mad at the way I'm being pressurised.

DELIA. I call it blackmail. By the way, is Viki out, too?

BILL. Yes. I checked when you went over to fetch the drink.
(Sighs as he sips his drink) But what am I going to do, Delia?

DELIA. There's a solution to every problem.

BILL. They've all made me feel such a complete heel.

(sighs again) I shall have to give up the whole idea of
going to Australia.

DELIA. Now, Mr. Mouse! *(She takes a drink from her glass)*
Actually, I think you've won already.

BILL. Won! It doesn't feel like it. You see, I love Joan —
and the girls, damn them!
*(DELIA lifts the whisky bottle and leans close to him
to top up his glass. He sniffs appreciatively)*

BILL. I say — that perfume! Mmm.

DELIA. I'm glad you like it. What was I saying?
*(DELIA replaces bottle. He goes on drinking, hardly
noticing he is doing it)*

BILL. You made the incredible statement that I'd already
won. I think you'd better explain.

DELIA. It's like this, Bill. You've won a tactical victory.
Joan believes she's lost. This last fling of hers —

BILL. That she's staying with the girls?

DELIA. Yes. She doesn't mean it. It was a desperation measure.

BILL. It's made me pretty desperate. I depend on her and she
knows it. If she forces me to go alone, I don't suppose I will. . . .

DELIA. Now, Bill, look at it this way. Joan doesn't want to lose
you either, so it all depends on who gives in first, doesn't it?

BILL. *(thinking)* Do you really think that's the situation?

DELIA. I'm sure of it.

BILL. It's true that Joan depends on me in lots of ways. . . .. .

DELIA. Go through all the movements of carrying on alone, and
she'll come running.

BILL. Delia, she's awfully obstinate. You don't know. Joan cuts
off her nose to spite her face.

DELIA. All right. Let's suppose Joan won't give in while you're
still here. . . . suppose you have to actually go alone. . . .

BILL. I'd simply hate that. I'd be so lonely out there. I don't
make friends easily you know.

DELIA. *(very gently and charmingly)* You needn't be alone, Bill.

BILL. How's that?

DELIA. Is Joan the only woman in the world?

BILL. *(Not seeing her trend at all)* You're not suggesting I find me a woman out there?

DELIA. Why not?

BILL. I wouldn't have the nerve.

DELIA. My crystal ball tells me one will be there, waiting for you.

BILL. You're pulling my leg!

DELIA. Do you remember, Bill, my saying I might visit my cousins in Australia?

BILL. Yes. . .

DELIA. Well?

BILL. *(illuminated)* You don't mean you are going — now — at once?

DELIA. I made a provisional booking by air yesterday.

BILL. *(delighted)* Delia! You're not kidding?

DELIA. No kidding. I'll be in Sydney two weeks after you arrive yourself.

BILL. Only two weeks! But that's great! Terrific!

DELIA. The steel works are only about an hour's rail journey from Sydney.

BILL. So I won't be completely without friends.

DELIA. If I'll do?

BILL. Do!
  (BILL takes her hand in both his and squeezes it)
  I can't think of anyone I'd rather have near me out there—except Joan, of course.

DELIA. Except Joan, of course.

BILL. Oh, I feel so much better!

DELIA. *(raising her glass)* Let's drink to our meeting Down Under.

BILL. *(raising his glass)* To our meeting Down Under!
  (They drink and replace their glasses on the table)

BILL. *(enthusiastic)* And you know, this news might make a difference to Joan's feelings. You're her best friend —

DELIA. *(dryly)* Oh, yes?

BILL. . . . . . don't you see, if you will be there while we're settling in, it could make all the difference . . . . . especially if you're right, and she's only making a last ditch stand.

(During this speech, DELIA looks at BILL with raised eyebrows. Can he be so dumb that he doesn't see what she is suggesting?)

DELIA. There's something in that. . . . . but perhaps not quite what you think.

BILL. What's that mean?

DELIA. Joan is jealous of me.

BILL. *(amazed)* Jealous?. . . . . . Oh, you mean mother-in-law catching us that time when I gave you a grateful kiss?

DELIA. It wasn't entirely grateful, was it, Bill?

BILL. *(bemused)* Delia!

DELIA. *(softly)* I hope not.

BILL. You *hope* – Delia! I – I don't know what to think.

DELIA. *(her face close to his, her lips inviting)* Don't you?
(BILL kisses her. She responds warmly. They go into a series of clinches, each warmer than the other.)

BILL. *(coming up for air)* Well! This is a turn up!

DELIA. *(snuggling into his shoulder)* You old silly. I've adored you for years.

BILL. *(preening himself)* You have?

DELIA. Yes – long before Stan died. Didn't you ever guess?

BILL. I thought you were Joan's friend.

DELIA. It was the only way I could keep close to you, Bill.
(Gazes up at him) A snake in the grass, that's me.

BILL. A most beautiful snake!. Why have I never noticed?

DELIA. Blinded by domesticity. I was in that state too, till you moved in next door. With me it was love at first sight.

BILL. Not when you came to complain about the broken fence?

DELIA. The previous owners would never do anything.

BILL. I mended it and drove a nail into my thumb. You were so kind.

DELIA. You didn't notice how my hands trembled as I bandaged your poor thumb?

BILL. No. I thought Joan bandaged it.

DELIA. I'll never forget it.

BILL. Three years ago! All that time wasted.

DELIA. We'll make up for it.

BILL. *(infatuated)* How?

DELIA. In Sydney. I'll get a flat, through my cousin —

BILL. The one in the estate business. . . . .

DELIA. Yes.

BILL. You promised he'd find me somewhere to live, too.

DELIA. Isn't one flat enough for the two of us?

BILL. *(intrigued but nervous)* Me — and you together?

DELIA. Why not? Until Joan joins you.

BILL. But — Delia, when she knows you're going to Australia on holiday, she may come too.

DELIA. Then we won't tell her till I actually go.

BILL. I see. *(thinking)* Do you think she'll *not* change her mind anyway, and come with me?

DELIA. If I have a flat in Sydney, and you have to come to Sydney on business — any kind of business — we can be together sometimes, can't we?

BILL. Yes. Yes. I'd see to that!

DELIA. And if Joan doesn't know about my holiday and sticks to her refusal to come out with you, then we'll have those glorious weeks together, alone.

BILL. Delia!

(They kiss again, BILL *in a dream of delight,* DELIA *very pleased with herself)*

BILL. I won't breathe a word!

DELIA. Nor I.

BILL. Is that why you're going to have the house done up now — while you're away?

DELIA. That's the idea.

BILL. You know, one thing bothers me —

DELIA. What's that?

BILL. I've heard the Aussies are very old-fashioned in their ideas. .. .. us living together, I mean.

DELIA. Easy. We're cousins. You are staying with me while you find accomodation for your wife and family.

BILL. Yes, I suppose that would go down all right.

DELIA. You're not backing out, Bill? Don't you like me as a
      lover?
BILL. *(grabbing her)* Like you! Try me!
DELIA. *(holding him off)* Not here, Bill.
BILL. At your place, then.
DELIA. The builder. . . .
BILL. Damn the builder. When?
DELIA. Steady on. How do I know you're serious?
BILL. About you?
DELIA. No, silly. . . . . about going alone to Australia.
BILL. I've accepted the job and I've told Joan, haven't I?
DELIA. Only a little while ago you said you'd given in and would
      stay here.
BILL. Not now. Not on your life. I'm going.
DELIA. Because of me?
BILL. Because of the most beautiful woman in the world.
DELIA. *(sits up, briskly)* That's settled then. And you'll give
      Joan her 'either/or' answer at once?
BILL. I thought I might keep her dangling for a bit.
DELIA. I need to be sure now. You see, I've got to make arrange-
      ments about the flat, haven't I?
BILL. Yes, of course. All right, I'll tell Joan I'm going on my
      own as soon as she gets back.
DELIA. Good.
BILL. Wouldn't it be awful if she gave in and said she'd come
      with me?
DELIA. Really, Bill – is that the loving husband speaking?
BILL. I didn't know about you then, did I?
DELIA. It was only a few minutes ago. And we say women are
      the changeable ones!
BILL. I must have loved you for ages – unconsciously.
DELIA. I'm glad you've woken up!
BILL. Me, too.
DELIA. About Joan – don't give her the chance to change her
      mind. Tell her you've got your air ticket –
BILL. But I haven't –

DELIA. That doesn't matter. You can get it tomorrow. Go into
    details of financial arrangements for her and the girls here —
BILL. That's a good idea.
DELIA. In fact, act as if you accept her plan to stay with the
    girls as the fairest and best one — for the girls. Avoid any
    opening she may give you for further discussion — and you've
    got her trapped in her own net.
BILL. *(admiringly)* Set a woman to catch a woman.
DELIA. You'll do it?
BILL. *(hesitating)* You're sure she'll follow me later?
DELIA. Do you want her to?
BILL. Delia — you put me in a devil of a spot.
DELIA. That means you do. *(laughs)* Don't look so upset. I'm
    not looking for a husband.
BILL. *(relieved)* You're not?
DELIA. *(touching his lips with her fingertip)* No.
BILL. *(catching her hand)* Delia, you're wonderful! I'm a lucky
    bastard!
DELIA. You'll tell Joan tonight — but not a word about my
    holiday?
BILL. I'll tell her — and not a dicky bird about you.
    *(BILL grabs her fervently, pushing her back on the settee so
    that they are both lying on it.)*
BILL. *ardently)* What more could a man want — beautiful —
    understanding — in a word 'with it'.
DELIA. *(mocking)* Oh, I'm with it all right . . . . . and it
    doesn't take a week to reckon you've been without it for some
    time!
    *(BILL laughs aloud, then sets to work to kiss her thoroughly.
    The room is now in semi-darkness, as no light has been put on.
    The door from the hall opens quietly and SAMANTHA appears
    a piece of paper in her hand. Muffled endearments and
    exclamations of delight come from the settee.
    SAMANTHA stares, puts a hand to her mouth and cautiously
    retires, closing the door quietly. The click reaches DELIA's
    ears. She sits up suddenly)*

BILL. *(nearly falling off the settee)* What's the matter?

DELIA. I heard the door. *(She switches on table light)*

BILL. I didn't

DELIA. I'm sure I did. *(She rises, smoothing her dress)* Come on, Bill, we'd better clear the glasses, I'll take the bottle and go.

BILL. No No. Don't leave me, Delia.

DELIA. I mustn't be seen here. It might spoil everything.

BILL. I can't wait. I want to be with you now and for always.

DELIA. You can, in Sydney — for a time, anyway.

BILL. I never thought I'd fall in love again.

DELIA. *(straightening her hair)* Better take the glasses to the kitchen and wash them.

BILL. One more kiss.

DELIA. Only one.

(they kiss. BILL *holds on to her)*

BILL. There's no one about. You were mistaken.

DELIA. I may have been.

BILL. Tell me again, did you really love me at first sight?

DELIA. Yes.

BILL. Blind idiot that I was.

DELIA. I must go now. Remember your promise.

BILL. Yes. You've given me the courage of a lion.

DELIA. That's my man. *(listens)* I think I was mistaken. One last drink, then.

(She pours the last of the whisky into the two glasses)

BILL. I'm tiddley already — not used to the stuff being a poor out-of-work chap.

DELIA. *(puts bottle on table and raises her glass)* To us. A short life and a merry one.

BILL. *(maudlin)* A long life, Delia!

DELIA. Well, who knows?

(They drink)

BILL. Perhaps when the girls are off my hands. . . .

DELIA. You would ditch Joan?

BILL. Perhaps she'll ditch me for some bronzed Australian sheep farmer.

DELIA. Perhaps she'll stay in England forever.

BILL. *(surprised at himself)* D'you know, I don't care any more
. . . . . as long as I've got you, my darling. I've never been so
happy. Never. Nothing can upset me now. Nothing.

(The front door opens and women's voices can be heard)

DELIA. Joan!

BILL. Worse. Mother-in-law!

*(BILL grabs DELIA's glass, takes a few steps to the kitchen,
realises it is not empty, swigs it and rushes on. DELIA picks up
the bottle, but does not know what to do with it as the door
handle rattles. She shoves it under the settee.*

*The door opens and MRS PASMORE appears, complete with
hat, coat, handbag and knitting bag)*

DELIA. *(warmly)* Hello there, Mrs Pasmore.

MRS PASMORE. You again. . . . .

*(BILL has just rinsed the glasses and is placing then quickly
in the cupboard when there is a loud shriek from the hall.
JOAN rushes in waving a piece of paper, followed by
SAMANTHA)*

JOAN. *(waving the paper at BILL)* It's all your fault!. . . . Oh,
what shall we do, what shall we do?

(She drops on to the settee and bursts into tears)

MRS PASMORE. Whatever is the matter?

SAMANTHA. It's Viki.*(Takes note from her mother)* Here you'd
better read it, Dad.

*(BILL takes the paper and reads. MRS PASMORE sits by her
daughter on the settee)*

MRS PASMORE. Pull yourself together, Joan!

JOAN. To think that I trusted him! Fed him, welcomed him in
my home!

MRS PASMORE. *(to BILL)* What does the note say, William?

BILL. *(handing her the note)* She's gone off to a Commune with
Chris.

MRS PASMORE. Gone to *Russia*!

SAMANTHA. No, Gran. A Community living place.

MRS PASMORE. Just what I expected. *(Hands note back to*

BILL*)*
JOAN. What shall we do?
BILL. Go after them, I suppose.
JOAN. *(hysterical)* It's all your fault — waltzing off to Matilda
  like that.
BILL. Who's Matilda?
MRS PASMORE. She's distraught. She means Australia.
JOAN. That's what I said.
MRS PASMORE. You didn't — but no matter.
  (DELIA has been standing aside, listening. She moves forward)
DELIA. You need a drink, Joan. Have you anything in the house?
  *(MRS PASMORE's foot strikes something under the settee.
  She bends down and finds the neck of the whisky bottle.)*
JOAN. Only some sherry. In the cupboard.
  (SAMANTHA runs across to the counter and opens a cupboard.
MRS PASMORE. *(placing whisky bottle on the table)* A pity this
  is empty.
JOAN. *(staring)* Where did that come from?
MRS PASMORE. Under the settee.
  (They look at BILL who mouths speechlessly)
DELIA. *(coolly)* I brought in a nip for Bill. I found him very
  depressed when I popped in to see Joan. It must have fallen off
  the table.
MRS PASMORE. So that's why the place smells like a distillery.
DELIA. *(sweetly)* You *do* get around, Mrs Pasmore. I've never
  been in a distillery.
  *(MRS PASMORE has no answer. SAMANTHA comes across
  with a glass and the sherry.)*
SAMANTHA. *(pouring some sherry)* There you are, Mum. Drink
  it up.
JOAN. *(taking glass)* But what are we going to *do*?
MRS PASMORE. I'd call the police if it was my daughter. I never
  did like that young man.
DELIA. She's not been gone an hour. I doubt the police would
  do anything.
BILL. They might send a constable to the nearest Commune,

wherever that is.

DELIA. Quite near — Furze Hill.

JOAN. But it could be a place hundreds of miles away. I wonder how long she has been gone?

SAMANTHA. She was here when I went over to Gran's and I was back in half an hour.

MRS PASMORE. You left at least ten minutes before we did, Samantha. Why didn't you give Victoria's note to your father? *(There is a slight pause. BILL and DELIA are on the alert)*

SAMANTHA. I didn't think it was that important.

JOAN & MRS PASMORE. *(together)* You didn't think!

SAMANTHA. I mean, they've a right to plan their own lives, haven't they? Viki is over the age of consent.

MRS PASMORE. She's not eighteen.

JOAN. Samantha's right, Gran — sixteen is the age of consent — outside marriage.

MRS PASMORE. Disgusting!

JOAN. I agree it's all wrong. How can a baby like Viki consent to a — a thing like this? It's that boy's fault — he ought to know better.

BILL. *(emboldened by the whisky)* Chris is eighteen and Viki is no baby.

JOAN. *(furious)* What do you mean by that?

DELIA. Bill means she's got her head screwed on. She knows what she's doing.

MRS PASMORE. All the more shame to her.

JOAN. Mum!

BILL. Shut up, you old bag!
(MRS PASMORE's mouth falls open and she is for once, bereft of words)

JOAN. Bill! *(she rises)* We must do *something*.

DELIA. Why not ring Chris's home? Find out if he's missing — if he told them anything.

JOAN. Of course! Delia, you're so practical. Bill, ring them please. I'm all shaky — I couldn't say a word, and I might be rude.

BILL. Of course. What's the number?

JOAN. What is it, Samantha?

SAMANTHA. 274 I think — or is it 724?

DELIA. We'll look it up. Come on, Bill.

(They exit to the hall. JOAN *sinks on to the settee again, and closes her eyes)*

SAMANTHA. More sherry, Mum?

JOAN. No thank you, dear.

(MRS PASMORE is clearly dying to talk to JOAN, *but cannot with* SAMANTHA *present. She searches in her knitting bag)*

MRS PASMORE. Samantha dear —

SAMANTHA. Yes, Gran?

MRS PASMORE. I'm sure I left a skein of this wool upstairs in one of the spare room drawers.*(Hands small ball of wool to* SAMANTHA*)* Could you find it for me? I shall need it soon.

SAMANTHA. Of course, Gran.

(SAMANTHA exits. Voices can be heard in the hall — as BILL *speaks on the 'phone)*

JOAN. You never left any wool here.

MRS PASMORE. I know. I wanted to ask you something, Joan.

JOAN. Yes?

MRS PASMORE. What do you think Bill was up to this afternoon — inviting Delia — and her whisky — in here immediately the house was empty?

JOAN. Oh, Mum — not that again. You seem to forget what I told you — Bill and I still sleep together.

MRS PASMORE. I've never heard that was a recipe for faithfulness.

JOAN. Besides — if they'd meant to get up to fun and games, Bill would have gone to her house.

MRS PASMORE. I'm wondering why he didn't.

JOAN. I'm much more worried about my Viki. It seems I didn't know Chris at all. I could have sworn he was a really nice, reliable boy.

MRS PASMORE. No woman ever knows the depths of a man's

depravity.

JOAN. Don't mum! I'm thinking what might happen before we can stop it. . . . . in a Commune they believe in free love. Viki and Chris will be *expected* to sleep together.

MRS PASMORE. If she had been brought up properly she wouldn't have listened to such a scheme. . . . . father behaving as he is.

JOAN. *(coldly)* You are speaking of my husband and my best friend. I haven't such a low opinion of people as you have.

MRS PASMORE. A pity. You might save youself some shocks.

(There is a hostile pause. JOAN *gets up and moves to the door)*

JOAN. I must know what's going on.

(As she reaches the door BILL *comes in followed by* DELIA*)*

JOAN. Any news?

BILL. None, I'm afraid. Chris is certainly out but he left no note and he doesn't seem to have taken any clothes.

(JOAN collapses on the settee again, weeping)

JOAN. Then they've gone!

(BILL sits on the settee beside her. She moves away from him angrily, fanning the air)

JOAN. Get away from me! It's all your doing with your mad idea of going to Australia. You've upset us all — and you're drunk too. Beast!

DELIA. *(cooling things down)* Shall we get the car out and go to Furze Hill?

JOAN. Yes, we could try.

BILL. *(rising)* Of course. I'll do it at once.

MRS PASMORE. You're not driving. William.

JOAN. No. I will.

DELIA. But you've been drinking too, Joan. So have I. *(to* MRS PASMORE*)* Mrs. Pasmore?

MRS PASMORE. I neither drink nor drive.

(JOAN gets up with determination, wiping her face and putting her handkerchief away)

JOAN. I've only had one little drink. I shall drive. And just wait till I get my hands on that Chris. After all the kindness I've

shown him — to seduce my darling daughter — take her away
to a beastly permissive Commune of drop-outs. . . . . I'll kill
him!

(The door opens and SAMANTHA *comes in followed by*
CHRIS, *looking very nervous. There is an amazed pause)*

SAMANTHA. I found him hanging about outside.

CHRIS. Excuse me — I did knock — then I found the door was
open. Samantha told me you were all here.

SAMANTHA. *(crossing to* MRS PASMORE*)* I couldn't find your
wool, Gran.

MRS. PASMORE. Never mind that now, dear.

*(*JOAN *recovers from her amazement and rushes towards*
CHRIS*)*

JOAN. Where's Viki? What have you done with her?

CHRIS. I do apologise, Mrs Tennant —

JOAN. *(screaming)* Apologise! You should be put in prison!

BILL. Draw it mild, Joan —

JOAN. Just let me get at him!

*(*CHRIS *shrinks away and* BILL *covers him)*

BILL. Shut up, Joan! *(She subsides. He speaks to* CHRIS*)* We
got a note from Viki to say she was running way with you,
Chris — to a Commune.

CHRIS. I know. I feel awful about it. I'm afraid she's still
waiting for me at Green Lane crossing.

JOAN. *(indignantly)* You left her there — all this time!

CHRIS. I'm sorry, really I am. But I felt I couldn't go through
with it. I should never have agreed in the first place.

(There is another amazed pause)

DELIA. It was Viki's idea?

CHRIS. Well, yes. She didn't want to go to Australia, you see. Of
course, I didn't want her to go either. But this seemed a bit
too much. . . . so I didn't go and meet her. I've behaved very
badly. I'm so sorry.

MRS PASMORE. I knew all along it was Victoria. I did warn you,
Joan, but no one ever listens to me.

CHRIS. *(going on)* I mean, Viki will soon be eighteen and we can get married — even if I have to come out to Australia and fetch her.

BILL. You won't have to, old chap. She's staying here with Samantha and their mother.

CHRIS. Oh, I say! I wish I'd known! Then all this was for nothing.

DELIA. It seems like it.

CHRIS. Gosh! I wish I'd known. Viki will be mad at me for standing her up.

MRS PASMORE. The best thing you ever did.

CHRIS. It would never have happened at all, Mr. Tennant if Mrs Tennant's plan to stop you going hadn't failed.

JOAN. *(very quickly)* What *are* you talking about, Chris?

BILL. So it was your idea, Joan — sending Chris to me to say he wouldn't let Viki go?

JOAN. *(giving in gracefully)* Poor children — they would have been broken-hearted if they'd been separated.

MRS PASMORE. Joan was quite right to try everything to bring you to your senses, William.

DELIA. *(coming forward)* Bill *has* come to his senses.

JOAN. *(rushing to him)* Oh, darling, you're staying after all! I knew you would! I knew you couldn't leave us!

BILL. *(trying to disentangle himself)* Just a minute — you don't quite —

(VIKI walks in and sees CHRIS)

VIKI. You!.... Why didn't you turn up?

CHRIS. Viki — I'm sorry, but — I thought —

VIKI. You thought! Wait till you hear what *I* think of you Chris Maitland!

JOAN. Now dear, it's all right —

VIKI. All right, is it?

CHRIS. Viki, I can explain —

VIKI. Don't you Viki me. I've never been stood up in my life before and this is the last time *you'll* get the chance.

CHRIS. But, Viki —

VIKI. I know. You let me down because you're chicken —

chicken through and through.

CHRIS. No, it wasn't like that —

VIKI. *(dramatically)* I'm finished with you! You haven't the guts of a louse and I never want to see you again! *(She points to the door)* Get out!

(CHRIS turns away miserably and slinks out)

BILL. *(to* VIKI*)* You forgot something.

VIKI. What?

BILL. 'Never darken my door again!'

(VIKI makes a furious gesture and turns her back on him)

DELIA. I think that was a bit hard, poor boy!

(DELIA exits after CHRIS)

JOAN. *(to* BILL*)* Now see what you've done!

BILL. What — me again?

SAMANTHA. *(to* VIKI*)* That was a bit steep, Viki.

(VIKI sits on the settee and bursts into tears. JOAN sits by her and puts an arm round her. MRS PASMORE goes to the window and peers out)

JOAN. My poor baby! *(Starts crying herself)*

BILL. *(after a pause)* When you've both turned off the taps sufficiently to hear me, I have an announcement to make.

(VIKI and JOAN dry their eyes)

JOAN. Well? Oh, you mean to tell the girls about your plans?

BILL. I'm telling the girls what is to happen, yes. This afternoon your mother told me that she would stay here to be with you two girls, so that you could finish your schooling. . . . . .

(VIKI suddenly radiant, gets up and hurls herself at her father)

VIKI. So we're all staying here after all! Good old Dad! Good old Mum!

SAMANTHA. That's a relief.

BILL. *(pushing* VIKI *away)* That's not the plan.

SAMANTHA. Not?

BILL. No. I'll be going to Australia alone.

(There is a moment's shocked pause, then JOAN *jumps up)*

JOAN. But Bill — I don't understand. . . Delia just said you'd come to your senses.

BILL. I have. *(he faces them)* I'm tired of being bossed about by all of you. . . . you too, mother-in-law. I'm doing what *I* want to do, looking after *my* future. You can all come out whenever you like. I'll see you have a home to come to.

(No one speaks for a few moments. VIKI looks indignant)

VIKI. It's not fair! I needn't have quarrelled with Chris. Now I've got to make it up with him.

JOAN. Yes, dear — you do that. He's a nice boy, you know. He couldn't bear the idea of you in that horrid Commune.

VIKI. I shall hold it against him for a long time.

JOAN. Yes, dear.

MRS PASMORE. If you want to catch him, he's talking to Delia Jones outside.

VIKI. Oh, is he?

(VIKI looks at herself in the mirror quickly and goes out with as much dignity as haste can muster)

BILL. Well, I hope that's all settled. Now, how about some tea? I'm starving.

SAMANTHA. Me, too.

MRS PASMORE. I'll be going.

JOAN. *(rather coolly)* You're welcome to stay.

MRS PASMORE. I've got a casserole in the oven which you and I were going to have.

JOAN. Of course. I forgot.

SAMANTHA. Sorry I couldn't find the wool, Gran.

MRS PASMORE. *(proceeding to hall door)* I may have taken it home. Good-bye.

(MRS PASMORE sweeps out)

SAMANTHA. Gran's upset. *(grinning at her father)* I'm not surprised after what you said to her.

BILL. Oh, Lord — I'd better go after her and apologise.

JOAN. Please do, Bill.

(BILL exits hastily)

Oh, dear, I've got such a headache.

SAMANTHA. Food will do you good.

(JOAN looks at herself in the wall mirror and tidies her hair)

JOAN. Do you think I look my age, dear?

SAMANTHA. Depends what your age is. It\varies a bit.

JOAN. Don't be silly. *(Looks round room)* You know, between ourselves, I'm glad your father isn't staying in England.

SAMANTHA. *(amazed)* Mum, what *are* you saying?

JOAN. I believe your Gran is right. Delia has been getting far too interested in him. Yes, he will be safer ten thousand miles away.

SAMANTHA. But mum — surely you know?

JOAN. Know what?

SAMANTHA. Alfie told me —

JOAN. The milkman's boy? Oh, yes?

SAMANTHA. Delia is leaving on the seventh for a holiday. In Australia.

QUICK CURTAIN
End of Scene 1

SCENE 2

A week later. Afternoon
(JOAN is walking up and down in agitation. MRS PASMORE is sitting knitting on the settee)

JOAN. Where can he be? *(MRS PASMORE does not reply)* You don't think he's with Delia?

MRS PASMORE. Where else?

JOAN. He might have gone for a walk — or to the swimming baths. Bill loves a swim.

MRS PASMORE. The baths are closed.

JOAN. Closed?

MRS PASMORE. Annual clean out.

JOAN. Oh. Well, no doubt he's taking a walk.

MRS PASMORE. It's a freezing March day. His overcoat is in the hall, and his jacket. I see his mac behind the kitchen door.

JOAN. He has other clothes upstairs.

MRS. PASMORE. Believe what you want to. He's next door, take it from me.

JOAN. *(dropping into a chair)* Oh, Mum — what am I to do? Was ever a woman in such a dilemma!

MRS PASMORE. It's a question of what you put first, isn't it?

JOAN. Bill or the children? Yes.

MRS PASMORE. I know my opinion is worth nothing, but I think its most important that the girls don't know their father is carrying on with another woman.

JOAN. But we don't know that he is!

MRS PASMORE. *(going on)* Especially a woman who is supposed to be their mother's best friend.

JOAN. I don't know what to believe. Delia has been perfectly frank about her holiday to see her cousins —

MRS PASMORE. Holiday, my foot. She'll stay out there as long as she wants, you see.

JOAN. But she's being so kind — getting her cousin to find him a place to live and — and —

MRS PASMORE. A love nest for two, no doubt.

JOAN. *(horrified)* How can you, Mum! She's staying with her cousins. I'm sure you're wrong about Delia. I really am.

MRS PASMORE. Well, be it on your own head. If you let him go alone, you've lost him.

JOAN. But the girls!

MRS PASMORE. The girls will have lost a father.

JOAN. Oh, no!

MRS PASMORE. That's my opinion, but no one ever listens to me. *(Pause)* Why don't you have it out with him when he gets in.

JOAN. What do you mean — have it out?

MRS PASMORE. Ask him about that woman straight.

JOAN. Oh, dear. . . . I suppose I could.

MRS PASMORE. You'll be able to tell if he's lying, won't you?

JOAN. Oh, yes.

MRS PASMORE. Good. Then do it.

JOAN. *(hesitating)* I could just climb down and change my mind and go with him.

MRS PASMORE. Without the girls?

JOAN. It would have to be without them. I can't upset everything we've arranged, and with Viki almost going into a decline because she doesn't know how to approach Chris after all she's said. . . . . well, I must give her a chance to make it up, mustn't I?

MRS PASMORE. Another one in the family who doesn't want to climb down. Well, make up your mind. You've either got to give in and go with him or tackle him about Delia Jones.

JOAN. But don't you see — either way I have to go with him and leave the girls.

MRS PASMORE. Then you *do* think he's not to be trusted with that woman?

JOAN. Oh, I don't know.

MRS PASMORE. Time you did. Stop putting your head in the sand, Joan.

JOAN. *(coming to a decision)* You're right, Mum. I'll tackle him.
 (MRS PASMORE puts her knitting away in her work bag and rises)
 You're not going?
MRS PASMORE. Yes, dear. My presence would only be an embarrassment to both of you.
JOAN. *(rising)* When shall I see you again?
MRS PASMORE. I'm always there, my dear.
JOAN. Bless you, Mum.
 (JOAN starts for the hall door to see her mother out, but MRS PASMORE moves towards the kitchen area)
MRS PASMORE. I'll go this way.
JOAN. But why? It's further round for you.
MRS PASMORE. I might just catch him sneaking out of *her* side door.
JOAN. Mum, you are dreadful!
 (But JOAN follows her mother and they both exit by the side door.
 After a few seconds the front door opens and shuts and voices are heard. VIKI and SAMANTHA walk in with their school cases. SAMANTHA flings hers across the room on to one of the arm chairs)
SAMANTHA. Whoops! End of term! Hurray!
VIKI. *(looking round)* No one here. *(She sits and sighs deeply)* No sign of Chris.
SAMANTHA. *(coming to the table and looking out of side of window)* Cheer up, It's only a week.
VIKI. A year!
SAMANTHA. *(interested at something she sees)* Why, there are Mum and Gran. They must have just gone out of the side door. *(VIKI turns and peers out of the window also)*
VIKI. What *are* they doing?
SAMANTHA. Looking into Delia's kitchen window. But why?
 (The girls look at each other, querying)
VIKI. Hoping to catch Dad and Delia at it.
SAMANTHA. In the kitchen? Very uncomfortable. I should

think.

VIKI. I didn't mean more than necking.

SAMANTHA. Go on. They're grown-ups. You don't suppoɪ
   they'd stop at necking. . . . . . . expecially after what I saw.

VIKI. That was on the settee. One doesn't in the kitchen.

SAMANTHA. I suppose anywhere will do if you're keen.

VIKI. I'm sure Dad wouldn't.

SAMANTHA. You know, I've always thought hay stacks must
   be very uncomfortable — itchy. *(looking out of window)*
   They've gone to the gate.
   *(*SAMANTHA *sits by* VIKI*)*   •

VIKI. Sammy, you don't seriously think Dad *would* — with
   Delia?

SAMANTHA. Have sex? *(*VIKI *winches)* With enough whisky and
   opportunity, why not?

VIKI. But he's our father.

SAMANTHA. Fathers are human, aren't they? I'd be very
   disappointed in him, personally, if he ran away from tempta-
   tion — like that milksop, Joseph.

VIKI. *(uneasily)* But so close to home. . . . . .

SAMANTHA. For a girl who going to run off to live in an
   unsanctified union with her boy friend —

VIKI. *(shocked)* No such thing!

SAMANTHA. *Wouldn't* you have had sex with Chris when you
   got there?

VIKI. Don't be so crude.

SAMANTHA. That's what it is. Having sex is like having breakfast.

VIKI. It wouldn't be with Chris and me.

SAMANTHA. What's so special about Chris and you?

VIKI. We love each other.

SAMANTHA. Is that why he cuts you dead when he sees you?

VIKI. *(ready to cry)* Don't be so beastly! He thinks I never
   want to see him again.

SAMANTHA. That's what you told him.

VIKI. But I didn't mean it. Oh, Sammy, I love him so much!

SAMANTHA. How do you know it isn't just sexual hunger?

(VIKI jumps up, bursting into tears)

VIKI. Because it isn't. I love him. I love him. But you wouldn't understand, you horrid little toad. It's awful — like being burnt up inside and all empty.

SAMANTHA. Sounds just like hunger to me. All right, I'm sorry. Blow your nose and sit down.

(VIKI blows her nose and sits down. SAMANTHA looks out of the window)

SAMANTHA. Mum's still talking to Gran at the gate. I wonder what she's going to do.

VIKI. About Australia?

SAMANTHA. Yes. She can't let Dad go off with Delia alone, can she?

VIKI. And she can't change her mind after saying she won't leave us.

SAMANTHA. That would be losing face. . . . Personally, I wouldn't mind if she went. I might even go with her.

VIKI. *(astonished)* Go with her? But your 'A' levels. . . . .

SAMANTHA. Australia sounds absolutely super for sport. Jane has been telling me about it.

VIKI. But Sammy — your career as a teacher?

SAMANTHA. I can do that anywhere. *(looks out of window)*

VIKI. But what about *me*?

SAMANTHA. There's Chris — outside.

VIKI. *(jumping up in agitation)* Oh, my face, my hair!
(She rushes across to the mirror)

SAMANTHA. There he is, the big daftie, mooning about, waiting for a crumb to fall from your table.

VIKI. Religious instruction has certainly got you, Sammy.
(turning) How do I look?

SAMANTHA. Same as usual. I'm not religious, mind you. I'm an atheist.
(There is a short ring at the front door)

SAMANTHA. Gosh, he's summoned enough courage to press the bell. Do you want me to and drag him in?

VIKI. Yes. What shall I say? I don't know what to say!

SAMANTHA. *(going to the hall door)* Apologise to him. He was entirely in the right, stopping you from making an idiot of yourself. Come *on*! I'll go to the bedroom and freeze in the cause of 'lerve'.

(SAMANTHA picks up her case of books off the settee. VIKI rushes to the hall door and follows her out)

(JOAN enters from side door with some daffodils from the garden. She puts them on the counter and comes down L She sees VIKI's books)

JOAN. *(to herself)* Oh, Viki's in.

(There are voices in the hall. JOAN snatches a bowl of fading flowers and hurries to the sink, emptying bowl and putting fading flowers in the bin under the sink. She puts fresh water into the bowl and sets it on the counter. As she arranges the fresh daffodils the door opens and VIKI comes in followed by CHRIS, who looks exceedingly nervous).

JOAN. *(flustered)* Hello dear. . . . . and hello Chris. Do come in. Nice to see you. Aren't the daffodils pretty? From the garden. *(She fills the vase and leaves it on the counter)* Now I must go upstairs. Will you stay to tea?

(JOAN comes round into the living room on her way to the hall. CHRIS looks at VIKI who makes no sign)

CHRIS. No thank you, Mrs Tennant.

JOAN. Well. . . . be seeing you, Chris. *(JOAN exits)*

(There is a fidgety silence, both standing.)

VIKI. You wanted to say something?

CHRIS. Yes. I'm miserable.

(VIKI makes a movement towards him, but checks herself)

VIKI. I should hope so.

CHRIS. If only you'd believe I did it for you.

VIKI. I'm supposed to be flattered you backed out of going away with with me?

CHRIS. No, of course not, But that wasn't the way to do it.

VIKI. Then why didn't you keep the date and tell me?

CHRIS. Because I knew you'd overrule me.

VIKI. *(stung, because it is true)* And if you're so weak, what can

I do but take the lead? You can't make a decision on your
own, Chris. You're still Mummy's boy, aren't you?

CHRIS. No, Viki —

VIKI. And to think I was considering tying myself to you for
life!

CHRIS. Oh, Viki darling —

VIKI. Not any more. Not while you are such a — a — milksop.

CHRIS. I'm not a milksop, Viki. I'm not really. I can prove it.

VIKI. How?

   (CHRIS takes a big breath)

CHRIS. I've got an assisted passage to Australia.

VIKI. (staggered) B — But why?

CHRIS. To be with you, Viki. I'll make good, you see if I don't
   It all happened because of this Aussie chap who came to visit
   us. He lives in Sydney and he's offered me a job in his office. . .
   its almost the same work that I'm doing now. . . . . Insurance.
   You see, his Dad was a war friend of my Dad's. . . . so I'm
   going. . . . . and Sydney is only an hour's journey from
   Newcastle, where your Dad will be working. . . . . Isn't it
   amazing?
   (CHRIS loses his breath and stops. Then he becomes aware of
   the silence and the odd way VIKI is looking at him)

CHRIS. Why, what's the matter Viki?

VIKI. (almost crying) But Chris. . . . I'm not going to Australia!

CHRIS. N — not going? Oh, Christ!

VIKI. Nor is Samantha. Nor Mum. Dad's going alone because of
   our schooling.

CHRIS. (groaning) What have I done?

VIKI. I think it's splendid of you, Chris.

CHRIS. You do?

VIKI. (putting a hand on his arm) I can fly out next summer, at
   the end of the school year.

CHRIS. (counting) Fourteen months! I don't think I could exist
   that long without you — alone — without friends. Besides, you
   might find someone else and forget me.

VIKI. And you might find another girl and forget me!

TOGETHER. How awful!
 (They stare into space tragically, hands clasped)
CHRIS. How can I get out of it? I'll have to break my leg or
    something. Might as well break my neck while I'm about it.
    (VIKI flings her arms round him, bursting into tears)
VIKI. Oh, Chris, please don't. I've missed you so much.
CHRIS. Viki darling — have you really?
VIKI. I can't let you go.
CHRIS. But how can I get out of it?
    (They cling together, thinking. Then VIKI has an idea)
VIKI. Chris, why shouldn't I go with Dad. *My* schooling isn't
    important.
CHRIS. What would your mother say?
VIKI. I don't care. It's our life. Dad will understand. And I can
    tell Mum he needs me to look after him, can't I?
CHRIS. It's a good iea. . . . . . Yes, It might work. Viki, you're a
    witch and an angel and I love you terribly.
VIKI. Darling Chris, I love you too.
CHRIS. We can be married as soon as you finish school.
VIKI. Yes. I might not even have to go to school. Who cares
    about 'O' levels? Not me.
    (The door opens and SAMANTHA looks in)
SAMANTHA. Can we — *(seeing them entwined)* Oh, sorry!
    *(VIKI and CHRIS turn to the door, hands linked, smiling
    happily)*
VIKI. It's O.K. Come in.
    *(SAMANTHA comes in followed by JOAN. Seeing their
    happy faces she rushes to them and embraces first CHRIS and
    then VIKI)*
JOAN. Dear Chris. I'm so happy you and Viki have made it up.
VIKI. *(dashing in with the news)* Chris is going to Australia, Mum
    — a smashing job, so I'm going too.
JOAN. What did you say, dear?
VIKI. Chris has a job in Sydney, so I'm going with Dad to be
    with Chris.
    (JOAN is taken aback, but tries to be tactful)

JOAN. But darling, it's all settled that the three of us stay here.

SAMANTHA. Excuse me while I faint. *(She flops on to the settee)*
It's on, it's off, it's on. . . . .

VIKI. And this time we're both off — with Dad. He doesn't
know yet, of course.

JOAN. But how did this happen, Chris?

CHRIS. A friend of my Dad's offered me a job — at least his son
did when he came to visit us. I've got an assisted passage, too.
You see I thought you were all going with Mr. Tennant, didn't
I?

SAMANTHA. You've been invisible for a week, Chris. Things don't
stay the same that long in this house — not at present.

JOAN. We'll have to think this over, Viki. No snap decisions.

VIKI. *(firmly)* I'm sorry, Mum. I'm going with Dad whatever you
say. I can look after him and finish my schooling just as well
as I can here.

JOAN. B — but you won't have anywhere to live.

VIKI. Delia is getting Dad a place — it can be big enough for me
too.

JOAN. *(desperately)* It's not possible, really. I can't allow it. You
can go later. . . . . the following year. . . . . that's the earliest.
(CHRIS and VIKI look very upset. SAMANTHA breaks in)

SAMANTHA. I've been thinking, Mum. I don't want to stay here
without Viki and you. . . . .

JOAN. But she isn't going, dear, nor am I.

SAMANTHA. Oh, yes she is. I can see she's made up her mind.
And so are you.

JOAN. *I'm* going to Australia? But I'm not.

SAMANTHA. Of course you are. You simply must go now that
your *best friend* is going as well as Viki.

JOAN. You mean Delia?

SAMANTHA. She *is* your best friend, isn't she?

JOAN. Yes, of course.

SAMANTHA. She'll be able to show us round — welcome us at
her cousins' place in Sydney whenever we want to go to town —
help us in hundreds of ways. I don't mind taking pot luck with

a school, really I don't. I'll work just as hard. Promise. And
Jane at school tells me the sport there is absolutely super — or
rather 'beaut'. That's the superlative over there.

VIKI. *(rushing to embrace SAMANTHA)* Dear Sammy — it would
be so much more fun with you. . . . . and Mum, of course.
You will come, won't you, Mum?

CHRIS. Please, Mrs Tennant.

JOAN. *(in a dither, but seeing an opportunity to change her
mind)* Really I. . . . Well, it does seem sensible now that Chris
has led the way.

(SAMANTHA leaps off the settee)

SAMANTHA. Australia, here we come!

(CHRIS and VIKI take hands delightedly)

JOAN. Now children, please!. . . . . There are a lot of things to
be thought about, for the moment, don't say a word to you
father

SAMANTHA. Of course not, Mum.

VIKI. *(winking at her sister)* We understand.

JOAN. *(explaining to CHRIS)* I don't want to raise his hopes too
soon.

SAMANTHA. *(low)* More likely to dash them.

JOAN. *(deep in thought)* What did you say, dear?

VIKI. *(quickly)* We were wondering about *cash*, Mum. Can we
afford it?

CHRIS. But you were going to get assisted passages, weren't you?

JOAN. Yes. I must go to the Travel Bureau at once. If we have to
wait too long for an air passage we may have to go by sea.

VIKI. We'll come with you, Mum Then we'll need a few clothes
We just haven't a thing to wear.

JOAN. Of course. After that your father must sign the
emigration forms. That's the moment to tell him.

VIKI. That's it! We'll surprise him!

SAMANTHA. We'll do that all right!

*(As they laugh together, the side door opens and BILL comes
in carrying some small parcels. They stop laughing but watch
him pass, broad grins on their faces. He notes this and is very*

uneasy.
At the hall door BILL *goes out half way, then looks back suspiciously. They all turn their backs, shaking with laughter.* BILL *stays there, staring and bursting with curiosity and suspicion.)*

CURTAIN.

SCENE 3

Two days later. A Monday mid-morning.
(MRS PASMORE and JOAN are seated having a cup of coffee
MRS PASMORE is knitting, as usual).

MRS PASMORE. So you never faced him with it?

JOAN. It wasn't necessary. As long as I'm with him, he's safe.

MRS PASMORE. H'm. It seems to me that Delia Jones can as
easily take you in in Australia as she does here.

JOAN. But she'll only be there six weeks.

MRS PASMORE. So she says.

JOAN. We've been friends for three years and I've never known
Delia lie.

MRS PASMORE. She knows how to keep the eleventh command-
ment, if not some of the others. I don't trust her.

JOAN. *(nettled)* You don't have to. I do hate the way you always
question my judgement.
*(There is a pause during which MRS PASMORE studies a
pattern book)*

MRS PASMORE. If you trust the woman so completely, why did
you find it necessary to change your plans and go with
William?

JOAN. *(too quickly)* I could see the girls were determined to go —
because of Chris.

MRS PASMORE. That's not the truth.

JOAN. Oh, Mum — don't bully me! You know perfectly well I
was only looking for an excuse to go with Bill. I only said I
would stay with the girls to try to make Bill give up the
whole idea of emigrating.

MRS PASMORE. Because of the girl's education—particularly
Samantha's, *I* thought. . . . but then, I'm always wrong.

JOAN. *(wriggling on the hook)* Well, I've had second thoughts
about the education in New South Wales. Australia House gave
me some very satisfactory information.

MRS PASMORE. That, unless I'm mistaken, was after you'd
    decided to go.

JOAN. Oh, no. I found out all about it the week before.

MRS PASMORE. *(smugly)* After we caught William and that
    woman together here, I suppose.

JOAN. Don't be so infuriating! I never wanted Bill to go alone.
    How many more times must I tell you that Bill and I love
    each other.

MRS PASMORE. Wiser to speak for yourself alone.

JOAN. It was all your fault anyway.

MRS PASMORE. I was waiting for that.

JOAN. Well, if I hadn't been so adamant about staying here, I
    wouldn't feel such a fool now, having to tell Bill we're all
    coming with him. I'd never have taken such a stupid stand but
    for you!

MRS PASMORE. I notice it's always my fault when things go
    wrong. You were the same as a child, I get no thanks at all.

JOAN. That's not fair, Mum. I never forget to thank you for all
    you do for us — nor do the girls.

MRS PASMORE. I don't want verbal thanks — except for the sake
    of politeness.

JOAN. *(sulking)* What then?

MRS PASMORE. *(taking out her handkerchief)* When you're old
    and alone you need affection and understanding. *(wipes her
    eyes)* But I suppose that's too much to ask.

JOAN. *(contrite)* Oh, Mum, don't be like that. You know how
    fond I am of you — and the girls love you dearly. *(Puts hand
    on her arm)*

MRS PASMORE. *(twitching away)* You've made me drop a
    stitch.

JOAN. Anyway, what are we quarrelling about?

MRS PASMORE. I don't know if you don't, I'm sure.

JOAN. When you come to think of it, it was hardly surprising
    Bill turned to Delia for sympathy, with me being so beastly
    to him.

MRS PASMORE. Sympathy? Delia Jones is about as sympathetic

as a boa-constrictor.

JOAN. *(laughing)* Really, Mum!

(there is a short pause)

MRS PASMORE. She's taken him shopping you say?

JOAN. Yes. She does know what is worn out there;

MRS PASMORE. After twenty years' absence I should have thought she was a little out of date.

JOAN. Oh, stop nagging, Mum. Delia is in very close touch with her cousins.

MRS PASMORE. Male or female?

JOAN. Male — *(she stops short)* Mum! They all have wives.

(MRS PASMORE sniffs significantly and goes on knitting)

MRS PASMORE. *(after a pause)* You're telling him today about the change of plan?

JOAN. I'd rather have left it longer, but I can't. Having a joint account at the bank has put me in a fix for money. I can't get a loan, you see. We've used all our savings.

MRS PASMORE. Surely the bank would forward you something against the sale of the house?

JOAN. Not without Bill's signature too.

MRS PASMORE. Oh, I suppose not. . . . . and you don't want him to hear about the sale till you've told him. *(looks at wrist watch)* Mr. Weeks from the estate agents should be here at any minute.

JOAN. It's such a relief to me that you will be here to see the sale of the house through, Mum.

MRS PASMORE. I'm glad I'm *some* use.

JOAN. *(ignoring this)* More coffee?

MRS PASMORE. Thanks.

(As JOAN pours the coffee, there is a ring at the front door. JOAN puts the percolater down and rises)

JOAN. That'll be Mr. Weeks. Help yourself to milk and sugar.

(JOAN exits to the hall. MRS PASMORE helps herself to milk and sugar.

There is a confusion of voices. The front door closes. VIKI and SAMANTHA rush in carrying several large paper shopping bags.

They are very excited and happy)

VIKI. Cothes, gorgeous clothes, Gran!

MRS PASMORE. Not now, girls — the estate agent is here.

VIKI. *(whipping a bikini top out of one of the bags)*
Isn't it fab? Like the colour?
(As VIKI holds the bra top to her JOAN comes in followed by MR. WEEKS. He is an elderly man, large and portly, very urbane in manner)

MRS PASMORE. I'll see it all later, Viki.

JOAN. Upstairs, girls.
(Giggling together, the two girls run out. We hear them pound up the stairs. JOAN shuts the door)

JOAN. Sorry about that, Mr. Weeks. They've just been shopping.

MR WEEKS. *(indulgently)* Pretty young girls need pretty clothes.

JOAN. My mother, Mrs Pasmore.

MRS PASMORE. Good morning, Mr. Weeks.

MR WEEKS. *(bowing slightly)* Delighted, Mrs Pasmore.

JOAN. You'll want to look round, I expect?

MR WEEKS. *(whipping out notebook)* Yes, if I may — Just a few notes on the state of decoration and so on. Then you can safely leave the sale to me and Mrs Pasmore. Shall I start here?

JOAN. If you wish. Do you need me with you?

MR WEEKS. Not at all necessary, thank you Mrs Tennant.
(MR WEEKS starts glancing round the room, touching the walls here and there, examining the window frame etc. The two women go on talking)

MRS PASMORE. You'll be arriving irto their winter, won't you?

JOAN. Well — their autumn — like our summer, Delia says, only hotter midday.

MRS PASMORE. Then you don't really need to bother with extra clothes, do you?

JOAN. The girls do — they haven't had anything new for two years, Mum. And they deserve a treat. I shan't bother myself except for something new to arrive in. The shopping is very good over there, Delia says.

MRS PASMORE. I can't imagine her male cousins tell her the

price of women's clothes.

JOAN. *(sweetly)* But their wives do.

(There is a pause while MR WEEKS *moves round the counter into the kitchen area.* JOAN *is lost in thought)*

JOAN. I've been thinking, mum — the one thing that worries me, quite apart from having to leave my home *(she looks round regretfully)* — is the idea of leaving you here without any of us.

MRS PASMORE. After six weeks I'll have Delia Jones. *(dryly)* What more could I ask for?

JOAN. *(laughing)* How you dislike her!

MRS PASMORE. Don't worry about *my* life. Worry about your own.

(MR WEEKS prances towards them, indicating the door to the hall)

MR WEEKS. I may go upstairs?

JOAN. Please. Anywhere.

MRS PASMORE. The girls are probably trying on their new clothes. I should knock, Mr. Weeks.

JOAN. The door on the right. Or you might get a shock!

MR WEEKS. I might indeed. *(He exits laughing)*

JOAN. *(resuming her trend of thought)* But seriously, Mum, if you do find life lonely we've gone, you can always come out to us.

MRS PASMORE. *(decidedly)* It would need an earthquake to shake me out of my little flat. I have friends, you know.

JOAN. I understand. *(sighs)* I shall *hate* leaving here — our first real home all the years we've been married.

(The side door opens and DELIA *comes in carrying two large paper shopping bags. Behind her comes* BILL *laden with two new leather travelling cases)*

BILL. *(low)* Gawd — look who's here!

(DELIA advances, smiling)

DELIA. Dear Mrs Pasmore! I'm always bumping into you!

MRS PASMORE. *(coldly)* I'm sorry, I'm sure.

DELIA. It's a pleasure. *(turning to* JOAN*)* We've done the necessary, and for very little, too — three shirts and two pairs of linen trousers.

(DELIA puts the carrier bags on the table. BILL dumps the cases)

MRS PASMORE. Expensive looking luggage.

DELIA. Gets you good service when you travel.

(DELIA opens one of the bags and takes out a shirt in a cellophane packet. JOAN crosses and examines the cases)

JOAN. They're very nice indeed. Much nicer than — *(stops short then continues)* — anything we've ever had before.

DELIA. *(holding up shirt in loud colours)* What do you think of this?

(DELIA holds it against BILL. The two women look at him)

MRS PASMORE. Vulgar.

JOAN. A little bright.

DELIA. It's what the Aussies wear in their leisure time. Matches Bill's eyes, I think.

JOAN. Makes him look like the morning after.

MRS PASMORE. *(low)* It probably is.

(The others ignore this. There is a ring at the front door. DELIA looks out of the window)

DELIA. A delivery van. What else have you been buying, Bill?

BILL. Nothing.

(As JOAN moves to the hall door, feet are heard running down the stairs)

SAMANTHA. I'll get it, Mum.

(The front door opens. BILL is now peering out of the window)

BILL. More suitcases! *(Turning to JOAN)* Joan, you didn't go and buy them for me, did you?

JOAN. I — er — bought some suitcases.

BILL. Then we'll have to send some of them back.

(The front door closes. JOAN has come downstage. Her mother signals to her that now is the time)

MRS PASMORE. *(urgently)* Now!

(DELIA has followed JOAN down)

DELIA. Now what?

MRS PASMORE. *(busily)* I've dropped a stitch.

(The door from the hall is flung open and VIKI *clad in a bikini and* SAMANTHA *dressed in a 'hot pants' suit, come in, each dragging a large, very snazzy piece of luggage)*

SAMANTHA. Look, Mum — aren't they super? *(sees her father)* Oh.

(Both girls put down the luggage and stand in front of it, not knowing what to say)

BILL. I like mine better *(He indicates his two cases)*

SAMANTHA. *(rattles on, not knowing the situation)* Isn't Mr. Weeks nice? He has a grand-daughter of sixteen and knows all about teenage fashions. He's been looking at what we bought, . .

MRS PASMORE. With you clad like that, Viki?

VIKI. He didn't mind.

BILL. I'll bet he didn't. But why new frocks? Have we come into a fortune?

(No one replies. BILL *comes downstage)*

What's going on, Joan?

(DELIA has sized up the situation at once. She at once turns it to advantage, coming down to join BILL *and* JOAN, *smiling)*

DELIA. Isn't it obvious? You've got your dearest wish, Bill.

BILL. *(puzzled)* I have?

DELIA. The family are coming with you.

BILL. Coming — *(he swallows hard)*

DELIA. Am I right, Joan?

JOAN. Yes, Delia — and it's all on account of dear Chris.

BILL. *(more bewildered)* Chris?

JOAN. Yes. He's got a job in Sydney, specially to be with Viki. He hadn't heard she was staying here, you see. So Viki decided to go with you, Bill — and then Samantha wouldn't be parted from her — so there wasn't much point in my staying by myself, was there?

(JOAN laughs girlishly and hugs her husband's arm)

DELIA. *(filling the gap)* Of course not.

JOAN. So we're all coming. Isn't it marvellous how things change!

BILL. It's bloody miraculous.

(The two girls hurl themselves on their father while JOAN *stands aside)*

SAMANTHA. I'm so excited, Dad. It's going to be beaut teaching the Aussies how to teach.

BILL. Oh, beaut!
(There is a tapping at the window, VIKI *looks and rushes to the door)*

VIKI. It's Chris! *(She exits)*

BILL. But *when* are you all going? And how? What about the fares?

JOAN. We've taken up the assisted passages they offered us. You only have to sign the papers.

BILL. I see. Good of you to tell me.

JOAN. We wanted to have everything settled and give you a big surprise.

BILL. You've done that.

JOAN. And now for the most delightful surprise of all. . . .
*(*BILL *lowers himself into an arm chair)*

BILL. I don't think I can take another.

JOAN. We've managed to book on the same flight as *you* have, Delia.

DELIA. *(dryly)* Well now, isn't that nice?

JOAN. We asked which you were on. There were vacant seats, so there you are. The three of us *and* Delia will arrive together only two weeks after you, Bill. Isn't that splendid?

BILL. But — you've — we've nowhere to live!

JOAN. That's where my friend Delia comes in. *(to* DELIA*)* Surely your cousin can find us somewhere, even if temporary, while we look for a house, dear? You can put Bill in touch with him and perhaps he can find accomodation during the two weeks he is there on his own.

DELIA. *(steadily)* Of course I can put him in touch. I was going to anyway. Something will be found for you all, I'm sure.

JOAN. That's what friends are for, isn't it, dear? And it's so reassuring to know that we'll have you to show us around, put us in touch with the right people and so on. We are indeed lucky to have such a friend.

SAMANTHA. Not half. *(She winks at her father)*
*(BILL, catching the wink, looks away in astonishment,
wondering how much his daughter know.
VIKI comes in with CHRIS. They are holding hands and
looking blissfully happy)*

VIKI. Mum — isn't it super! Chris has got a seat on our flight too.

BILL. *(acting dismay, to cover his really dismayed feelings)* Good
Lord, it'll be just like home! It only remains for mother-in-law
to heave anchor and we shan't know we've moved!
(They all laugh)

JOAN. That's not likely. Mother has just said it would take an
earthquake to move *her!*
(Very heavy feet are heard thudding down the stairs)

BILL. Is that a tremor?
(JOAN goes to the door, laughing, and opens it)

JOAN. No, it's Mr. Weeks, the estate agent, He's looking over the
house to sell it. Come in, Mr. Weeks.
*(MR WEEKS comes prancing in, full of good humour. DELIA
has turned her back and seems busy putting the shirt back
in its cellophane wrapper. MR WEEKS smiles at BILL, then
sees DELIA. He advances to her)*

MR WEEKS. Why, it's Mrs Jones, isn't it?
*(DELIA is forced to turn round. MR WEEKS snatches one of
her hands and presses it warmly in both his)*

MR WEEKS. *Dear* Mrs Jones. I was going to pop in now and see
you about the sale of *your* house — quite an exodus round
here. *(Laughs)* But I'll come in this afternoon, seeing you're
busy. Will that do?
*(There is a rapid exchange of looks all round, ending on MRS
PASMORE's triumphant smile as she nods at her daughter.
BILL and DELIA merely look somewhat guilty)*

DELIA. *(recovering her cool)* That will do nicely, thank you,
Mr. Weeks.
*(There is silence as MR WEEKS crosses to the hall door.
JOAN moves to go with him but MRS PASMORE rises*

quickly and forestalls her)

MR WEEKS. *(At the door)* Good-bye all.

MRS PASMORE. I'll see you out Mr. Weeks. There are things we must discuss — about the sale.

MR WEEKS. Of course. After you, dear lady.

(MRS PASMORE exits followed by MR WEEKS. The door closes. DELIA continues to put the shirt back in its cellophane cover, chatting airily)

DELIA. I was just going to tell you, Joan dear. I fixed yesterday with my cousins that I am to make my home permanently in Sydney. Now that I am alone in the world it seemed sensible. *(turning to JOAN with a charming smile)* Though, mind you, it would have been a wrench to leave you here. However, I knew it was only for a while, and now it turns out we'll not be separated at all. Isn't that wonderful?

SAMANTHA. Beaut.

(JOAN recovers her powers of speech)

JOAN. Absolutely splendid, Delia. We can be together all the time.

DELIA. Not quite so often, dear — I shall be in Sydney. But it means *any* of the family can have a home in Sydney any time they want to come to the big city.

VIKI. Gorgeous! I'll be able to see Chris often, won't I?

CHRIS. And I can come and spend week-ends with you, can't I, Mrs Tennant?

JOAN. Of course you can, Chris.

(All this time BILL has stood aside, not saying a word, though he puts on a false smile whenever he catches JOAN's eye.

The door opens and MRS PASMORE comes in looking singularly pleased with herself)

JOAN. Mr Weeks is satisfied with the arrangements, Mum?

MRS PASMORE. He's delighted.

(DELIA comes downstage and stands by BILL, but speaks to MRS PASMORE)

DELIA. I was just saying, Mrs Pasmore — that everything has

turned out for the best. We shall all be together as before. I'm
so happy. Aren't you Bill?

*(DELIA smiles at him, putting one hand behind her back where
the others cannot see. He grabs her hand, brightening visibly)*

MRS PASMORE. He should be. He's got everything a man could
want, haven't you William?

(BILL starts guiltily and drops DELIA's hand)

BILL. Er — have I?

MRS PASMORE. A good job, your family with you, not to
mention the family friend. . . . . and a bit more besides. . . . .

BILL. *(suspiciously)* A bit more what?

JOAN. What do you mean, Mum?

(There is the merest pause)

MRS PASMORE. I've just instructed Mr. Weeks to sell my flat
too.

JOAN. Sell your home!

VIKI. You're coming too! Good old Gran!

*(The two girls rush to their grandmother with exclamations of
delight)*

MRS PASMORE. Yes. I shall be joining you all just as soon as I
can.

SAMANTHA. You're a beaut!

MRS PASMORE. *(firmly)* I am neither old nor a beaut.

(The girls laugh. No one else does)

JOAN. But Mum — what happened to make you change. . . . .
(Her voice trails away as she looks at DELIA) . . . your mind?
(MRS PASMORE looks directly at DELIA)

MRS PASMORE. There must have been an earthquake — not a
hundred miles from here.

(The girls laugh again. No one else does)

*(There is a significant pause, then DELIA takes JOAN's arm
and BILL's and draws them both close to her, smiling from
one to the other)*

DELIA. It's just one thing on top of another, isn't it?

*(JOAN and BILL peep at each other across DELIA and look
front, a large question mark written on their faces)*

FURNITURE

Living-room: Large modern style settee
Two matching arm chairs
Coffee table with lamp (practical)
Bookcase
Desk with chair
Long dining table
5 matching chairs
Cushions for suite and window seat

Kitchen: Electric cooker
Electric kettle (practical)
Sink unit
Upright chair
Cupboard with built-in frig
Back door mat

Counter dividing two areas has cupboards on
living-room side with small drawers above.
One drawer and one cupboard door must be
practical.

LIGHTING

The apparent sources of daylight are from three windows: the
bow window up C., the unseen window on the fourth wall
looking out on to the garden: and the kitchen window over the
sink.

Artificial lighting is apparently a centre light in the kitchen, a
modern chandelier centre of living-room and a table lamp on
the coffee table down R.

PROPERTIES

ACT 1

Scene 1.   Everything for breakfast table for four
            Jacket with inner pocket (Bill)
                Two letters
            Morning newspaper (Bill)
            School blazer and beret (Samantha)
            Papers in long envelope (Bill)
            Mac and headscarf (Joan)
            Notepaper, envelope and pen in desk
            Nine pence (Bill)
            Hat, coat and shopping bag (Mrs Pasmore)
            Macs and coats for hall hooks.

Scene 2   Knitting bag and knitting (Mrs Pasmore)
            Afternoon paper (Bill)
            Three cups of tea
            Knives, forks and spoons for table
            Place mats
            Large salad bowl and salad
            oil, vinegar and cruet

Scene III   School blazer (Viki)
            Two school cases and extra books (girls)
            Mac and heavy shoes (Joan)
            Old dirty mac and wellingtons (Bill)
            Three cups and saucers
            Tea bags, sugar, milk
            Afternoon paper (Bill)
            Coat (Delia)

ACT II

Scene I   Coat (Delia)
            Bottle of whisky
            Two glasses
            Pieces of paper (note — Samantha)
            Bottle of sherry and glass
            Small ball of wool, knitting bag and

knitting (Mrs. P.)
Handkerchief (Joan)

Scene II Man's mac (on kitchen door)
Tow school cases
Daffodils (Joan)
Small parcels (Bill)

Scene III Knitting bag, knitting and pattern book (Mrs. P.)
Handkerchief (Mrs. Pasmore)
Coffee tray for two, with sugar and milk
    Notebook (Mr Weeks)
    4/5 large paper shopping bags, full (girls)
2 large shopping bags (Delia)
2 large new suitcases (Bill)
2 other new suitcases (girls)
Gay shirt in cellophane (Delia)
Hot pants suit (Samantha)
Bikini (Viki)

REHEARSAL DATES

CAST NOTES